COMMUNITY OR GHETTO?
An analysis of day centres
for single homeless people
in England and Wales

Jacqui Waters

The housing campaign for single people
September 1992

First published September 1992
by CHAR - the housing campaign for single people
5-15 Cromer Street, London WC1H 8LS
CHAR is a company limited by guarantee and a registered charity

© 1992 by Jacqui Waters. All rights reserved.
The moral right of the author has been asserted.

British Library Cataloguing-in-Publication Data
A catalogue record for this book is available from the British Library

ISBN 0 906951 33 X

Edited by Rupert Chandler
Design by Pat Kahn
Layout by Katrina Phillips
Printed by Unwin Brothers Limited, Surrey GU22 9LH

Contents

Acknowledgements vi
Foreword vii

Prologue **THE AUTHOR, THE THEMES, THE AIMS** 1
What sort of report? 1
The author and the themes 2
Questions and aims 3

Introduction **KEY POINTS IN UNDERSTANDING DAY CENTRE PROVISION** 6

Chapter 1 **WHAT IS A DAY CENTRE?**
Definitions, historical development and current models 10
**Towards a working definition;
common characteristics and core concepts** 11
The history and evolution of day centres 14
The traditional day centre and its origins 14
The evolution of day centres 15
The new style day centre 17
Role and aims 18
The spiritual/missionary approach:
a place of containment and acceptance 19
The social work approach:
a place of rehabilitation and change 20
The community work approach:
a place of empowerment and resource 21

iv Community or ghetto?

Chapter 2 **WHO USES DAY CENTRES AND WHY?**
The experience of the safe haven 23
Important trends 23
Second class services? 24
Dry pubs for the poor? 25
The welcome 26
Main reasons for day centre usage 28
Target user groups 31
Image and exclusions 32
The prevailing culture 34

Chapter 3 **THE HOLISTIC APPROACH: COMMUNITY OR GHETTO?** 37
The significance and meaning of community 38
Community or ghetto? 38
Community centre: a fantasy? 39
Community centre for homeless people? 40
User participation or empowerment 42
The voice of users 43
Them and us: the conflicts between staff and users 44
Creative involvement 45
Diversity of user groups: positive mix? 47
Equal opportunities 47
Mental health 51
Physical health 52
Income and employment 53
Prison and offending 53
Housing situation 53

Chapter 4 **RESOURCES TO FULFIL AIMS**
Funding, staffing and buildings 56
Funding 56
Monitoring/evaluation 56
The impact of funding on practice 58
Staffing 60
Management structures 60
Paid staff and conditions of service 61
The recruitment of staff 63

Use of volunteers 64
Outside services 65
The building 65
Ownership 66
Design 66
Building based services 67

Chapter 5 **SOME WAYS FORWARD**
Summary and conclusions 68
Time for review 68
Brief summary and conclusions 69
Definitions and main concepts 70
History and development 70
The safe haven 71
Community or ghetto? 72
Resources: funding, staffing and buildings 73
Closing thoughts 75

Appendix 1 **PROJECT PROFILES** 79
The Deptford Centre 80
Emmanuel House Day Centre 84
The Fanon Project 88
Minshull Street Day Centre 92
New Horizon Youth Centre 96
New Street Day Centre 100
SASH Day Centre 104
St. Botolph's Crypt Centre 108

Appendix 2 **THE RESEARCH BRIEF** 112
Background 112
Development of the research 113
The fieldwork 114

Notes 116
References 118

Acknowledgements

This report is based largely on the views and experiences of day centre users and workers, and I thank everyone involved for your honesty, time and participation. My particular thanks to users, volunteers and staff at the following day centres: the Deptford Centre, Emmanuel House, the Fanon Project, Jude Street, Minshull Street, New Horizon, SASH, and St Botolph's.

I hope that 'Community or Ghetto?' will go some way towards drawing attention to the important role played by day centres and towards informing the empowerment of users and staff.

The advisory group provided much valued direction, ideas and support in the course of the project which was not without controversy and challenge. My appreciation to: Isabel Anderson, Ian Boulton, Richard Goddard, Helen Pinch, Liz Pritchard and Peter Walker.

The report was funded by the Joseph Rowntree Foundation, and I would also like to acknowledge the role of CHAR in initiating this research.

The Resource Information Service (RIS) helped greatly in the format and design of the project profiles. Rupert Chandler from RIS additionally edited the report with consideration and a positive approach to the work.

Many other individuals and organisations made valuable contributions, especially the following: Central London Housing Advisory Service, Consortium, Drink Crisis Centre, Federation of Independent Advice Centres, Michael Fielding, Homeless Network, Pat Logan, Des Stockley and Thames Reach Housing Association.

*Don't panic, especially when a Vogon Commander reads his poetry to you...*My profound thanks to all of you friends, family and colleagues who endured endless discussions and drafts and who helped me not to panic. I am particularly indebted to Ian Boulton, Sharon Bye and Mike Comley for your creative thinking, encouragement and personal support.

Jacqui Waters

Foreword

If you are concerned about the homelessness crisis in this country, and particularly if you have some responsibility for providing services for homeless people, this report makes several demands of you.

It asks you to question some of the basic tenets on which those services are built. It accepts that the response to homelessness in England and Wales comes primarily from the voluntary sector but asks us to examine in detail what that means. What do these agencies believe in? What is their history? How do they treat people? Will they assist in change or do they have an interest in maintaining the status quo? It's hard to imagine another area of social policy being handed over to a variety of charities without us being a little curious about the answers to these questions.

'Community or Ghetto?' concentrates on what is perceived as the less sophisticated end of voluntary sector. It examines the opinions and experiences of workers and users of day centres for single homeless people. Some of you may feel, after reading this report, that their reputation is justified. But, if you are involved in direct housing provision, advice work, funding or campaigning, try to resist the temptation to feel smug or complacent and remember that we are all, whether we like it or not, part of the same strategy. We need to ask: is it working?

Agreeing on the approach, style and tone of this report was not an easy task. It had to be accessible, yes, but did that mean to all homeless people? It had to be provocative, but would it offend and upset people? It had to put forward firm views, but what if it was too opinionated? The advisory group for this research agonised over these questions but we need not have worried. The only decision we needed to make was to trust in the integrity and commitment of the researcher. Jacqui Waters has produced a highly readable, argumentative report which doesn't patronise those people who helped in its compilation. She has recognised the need for change but has refused to be dogmatic about how this is to be achieved. She has placed equal value on the experiences of the homeless and the housed; and where it was necessary to apportion blame for the shortcomings of voluntary sector daytime provision for homeless people, she has refused to point the finger at the powerless. 'Community or Ghetto?' leaves us all with a share of the responsibility.

Having worked in a day centre for eight years, I am confident that the research accurately and fairly portrays the experiences of day centre users and workers. I believe there will be a general feeling of relief that these experiences have been validated and the difficulties of their jobs and lives have been recognised for the first time. Perhaps the report will act as an irritant to those who don't want to examine too closely how fragile the structures which maintain social control really are. I hope it does.

This report is a positive alternative to a conventional piece of research. There aren't reams about data analysis, objectivity and methodology. There are no such mysteries to unravel here to get to the heart of the argument. Its refreshing honesty and readability will, I believe, prove to be its major strengths as a campaigning document.

And that is the main purpose here: to enliven the discussion around daytime provision and to add impetus to the campaign to improve it. 'Community or Ghetto?' certainly leaves CHAR and the rest of us no excuses for not getting on with it.

Ian Boulton
No Fixed Abode

PROLOGUE

The author, the themes, the aims

What sort of report?

When I first embarked on this research project, many people confirmed my understanding that it would be 'opening a can of worms'. The report, which is about day centres for single homeless people, touches on all the major issues and debates that affect everyone with any involvement in the single homeless field. It is aimed at an audience wider than this. In essence, it looks at one particular aspect of the way in which we treat each other living in Britain in 1992. It is about class, money and power; discrimination, social injustice and inequality; bigotry and parochialism. It is about how we all feel at some point of our lives - but some more than others: lonely, powerless, poor, unfulfilled and unsupported.

The report is therefore not a good practice guide that attempts to prescribe; nor an academic or scientific exercise that attempts to quantify. It is an exploratory discussion of services which have been largely ignored and marginalised, and which present us with challenges and questions that are complex and disturbing.

Research is often presented as objective truth or reality. Researchers are professionals who apply scientific detachment to their subject matter and call this process methodology. Researchers are extraordinary people who are able to discard the circumstances of their birth and upbringing, their value systems and prejudices, and who give the rest of us insights, usually into where we are going wrong. They appear not to be bound by contracts, salaries or competing vested interests. Research is somehow conducted in a vacuum that removes it from the political world in which the rest of us live. Much research goes unread or ignored.

This piece of writing records the findings and observations of a voluntary sector worker who was paid to go out into the world of day centres and report back on what was happening. It is the outcome of a three way contract between CHAR (the Housing Campaign for Single People) who commissioned the report, the Joseph Rowntree Foundation (JRF) who funded it, and myself as fieldworker/writer (see appendix 2).

I make no claims to be detached or uninvolved. I hold strong views about what I believe to be right and wrong in this world, and that is why I applied for this job. I believe that it is wrong that day centres for single homeless people should have to exist, and specifically in the shape that many of them currently do. I believe that this is a view shared by many of those who work in or use them.

The project has been guided by my interpretation of my task as an attempt at honest enquiry. Independence of mind and attitudes do not equate with detachment. But I have tried to do justice to the diversity of opinions, experiences and beliefs of the considerable number of people I consulted about the project. Writing inevitably involves a process of selection and exclusion. Just as it is an aim to convey to people who work in day centres that they cannot and should not try to achieve the impossible, so I have made choices and decisions that will not please all people. The report is a vessel for the voice of day centres, but my voice is there throughout.

The author and the themes

'My Universe is my eyes and my ears. Anything else is hearsay.'[1]

Having worked in aspects of single homelessness for several years, my particular interest in day centres was influenced by two work experiences. Firstly, as a member of the action research project that produced the report 'Sleeping Out in Central London', I was struck by this finding: that a sizeable proportion of our 'street' contacts continued to centre their lives around the people and institutions of the homelessness scene after being apparently successfully rehoused, rehabilitated and resettled.[2]

By far the majority of people wanted a place of their own and privacy. The evidence was, though, that loneliness, continuing stigma and poverty remained major problems once that aim had been achieved. For many others, the prospects of achieving the aim were too daunting. For a lot of people, housing did not mean an end to homelessness, and continued usage of soup runs and day centres testified to that. This has proved to be a major theme in my discussions with people involved in day centres, and one of the principal reasons why they exist.

Secondly, I worked in a project founded in the '60s as a supportive club for people discharged from prison and from psychiatric hospitals. By the late '80s, the project had developed a housing function which, backed by revenue funding, dominated the organisation, with the club limping along as the poor relation. I was employed to facilitate the introduction of housing for a new client group - single homeless women from a variety of backgrounds. This sharpened staff dissatisfaction with what appeared to be an anachronistic service, catering for a small group of mainly white men with a particular experience of homelessness.

The debates that ensued over who the project should be aimed at and what services should be delivered were often vitriolic and highly divisive. Some argued passionately that the club should change or close. Others argued equally strongly that it should stay as it was because it filled a gap for people who had nowhere else to go. In these arguments, which coalesced around interpretations of equal opportunities, the people who used and staffed the club had no say. For them, the increased professionalism of the project did not mean access to greater opportunities. I was profoundly uneasy at the part we, as staff, played in a process which effectively disempowered some of the people we were in the business of trying to empower.

This highlights further themes: the marginalisation of day centres compared with the residential sector; and what we mean by good practice and equal opportunities.

Returning to day centres felt like returning to a different world. Many things had changed, but many had not. I re-introduced myself to people who were still on the streets after eight years, and for whom life had actually got worse. That poses an immediate challenge. Why are they still there? I had to steel myself to walk into many day centres. They were still on the whole overcrowded, uncomfortable to be in and dominated by men. There were more day centres and more differences between them. But then, there were more people using them and greater visible diversity in the breadth of groups affected by homelessness. As one centre worker stated: *'I never thought the problem of homelessness could actually get any worse than when I started here'*.

The fundamental change was the political and economic climate over the last decade, which saw the government ascribe a key role to the voluntary sector in removing the problem of visible homelessness, whilst simultaneously cutting resources available to the statutory sector to provide housing and related community services. This has happened against the background of a reported increase in the levels of violence affecting people using and working in day centres. I believe that this violence is often the symptom of anger and impotence, resulting from the conspicuous disparity between those who have and who aspire to more and those who do not have.

I was relieved to meet some other people, homeless and housed, who also felt like dinosaurs from an era where individuals shared the belief that they could and should exercise some power, register protest against what is clearly unjust, and talk about morality without shame or apology.

Questions and aims

Projects that are defined in this report as day centres are frontline services in contact with people who do not have access to the rights and services that the housed and waged take for granted. Day centres exist as surrogate home and community to people who should be able to find these in mainstream society. The impulse behind the founding of day centres is rooted in concepts of hospitality and sanctuary, which are at least evident in early Christian history. They are places of shelter in the face of an uncaring and hostile world.

In the process of opening my can of worms, I found that many people had strong views about day centres. Many believed that most of them should be closed down. The real 'professionals' could then get on with the priority task of providing bricks and mortar housing. Those who believed that day centres have an important role to play could not agree on what it was or how a strategic pattern of services should be structured. Such people were often clearer about what services should not be: Victorian and Dickensian were terms that I heard a lot and used myself. But what will then happen to all these people who have nowhere else to go for food, rest, companionship etc? I was reminded of the debates and dilemmas that preceded the closure of large residential institutions (including psychiatric hospitals) and that have not yet taken place publicly in the non-residential field.

An aim of this report is to provoke such a debate, so that we can begin to establish minimum standards to protect the rights of both service users and providers. Such a debate can only take place within a framework in which ideology informs rather than intimidates. The field of day centres is bitterly divided, especially across London if only because of the greater numbers and range there. At SHIL's conference for London day centres in October '91, delegates could not even agree on whether it was a good idea to meet again and discuss their work.[3]

I do not believe that this situation will change unless people who work in church crypts handing out soup and shoes to white homeless men, and those above ground distributing a secular orthodoxy, start talking less defensively to each other about what they are doing, to whom and why. Homeless people have to be involved fully in this process. I believe that this has to happen before we can establish any framework for that elusive product that is bandied around as 'good practice'.

It seems fair to assume that workers would not be doing what they are, or believing what they do, unless they thought this went some way towards addressing the social problem of homelessness. Whether we agree or disagree, this has to be the starting point of discussion.

It is not the intention of this report to make prescriptions that are demoralising or unrealistic, and that set people up to fail or to feel unfairly criticised. However, other consumer based research, such as that produced by Good Practices in Mental Health, has highlighted five principles of good practice. They are:

- participation
- individuality
- respect
- information
- choice.[4]

These basically enshrine the right of people, in this instance people who use day centres, to lead ordinary and satisfying lives if they want to:

'Services can support people in achieving this through working with them to obtain resources and information that many of us take for granted: ordinary housing, benefits advice, use of community facilities, a source of income, friends and so on'.[5]

These are the foundation principles that are shared by many of the people I met in day centres but which are so difficult to implement. This is implicit to the text of this report.

What is clear is that day centre users will not go away. Their numbers are increasing and the platitude that homelessness and poverty threaten each and every one of us is ever more real. Day centres stand as a reminder of this. That, in my view, is why they have been largely ignored and what this report aims to go some way towards redressing.

I ask the reader to take seriously the challenge of single homelessness and to be prepared to do something about it. For people who are homeless and those providing services for them, this means at times saying a collective 'no' to funders, employers and governments. For people who give money and who make decisions that profoundly affect the lives of others, it means exercising imagination and intelligence, so that decisions improve rather than oppress the lives of the rest of us. For Joan and Joe Public, it means accepting homelessness for what it is: a circumstance that could happen to any of us.

INTRODUCTION

Key points in understanding day centre provision

This report addresses five main questions:
- What is a day centre? (Chapter 1)
- Who uses day centres and why? The concept of safe haven. (Chapter 2)
- How do centres respond to their users? The concept of community. (Chapter 3)
- What resources are available for the achievement of aims? Funding, staffing and buildings. (Chapter 4)
- What is the way forward for day centres? Summary and conclusions. (Chapter 5)

Day centres make day centre users just as hostels make hostel dwellers. Many homeless people feel stigmatised by and remain trapped in the services that we set up for them. Many homeless people would prefer not to have to use the services that we set up for them. The fundamental question which then follows is whether day centres equip people to deal with the outside world on equal terms, or whether they perpetuate the negative class status of their users, by creating a ghetto community that tries to meet their every need.

'A loose network of organisations, many...with their origins in church concern, who scrabble around each year to cobble together the funding to keep going. Many of whom operate from dilapidated, cramped, insanitary and difficult to find premises and on short insecure leases...staffed by often highly skilled and experienced people with little job security and no discernible career prospects.'[1]

Non-residential services are one of the least well defined aspects of single homelessness provision. Day centres for single homeless people are still widely viewed and treated as the unprofessional and Cinderella subsidiary of direct housing provision. There has been no previous research undertaken on a formal or wide scale basis in this field. In Britain, research has been largely limited to: internal organisational reviews; student placement dissertations; local directories of a mixture of daytime services; feasibility studies and so on. There are very few second tier policy, training and campaign bodies that have focused on day centres.

Day centres have evolved pragmatically and rapidly, over the last decade in particular. This evolution has taken place on an ad-hoc basis, 'subject to individual whims and quirks and funding availability. We are having to respond to increasing pressures without any model to compare with.'[2] This was a common concern amongst day centre staff - particularly outside London: 'day centres for homeless people are few and far between, especially outside London. There are few "role models" (good or bad!) to follow, and to a great extent policy evolves from experience.'[3]

Day centres are front-line services that are often the first point of contact for people in some sort of crisis. In common with other crisis services, day centre workers tend to be caught up in the day-to-day operation of delivering services, and lack the opportunities to step back and take a strategic view of their individual project in relation to others. This has contributed to a confusing assortment of services, some of which call themselves day centres and others which disassociate themselves from the various images evoked by the term. There are consequently no widely recognised definitions, or models with guidelines for service delivery - practice and evaluation.

Day centres for single homeless people have been largely the domain of the voluntary sector. The latter has always prided itself on the range and diversity of its provision and on its ability to respond imaginatively and immediately to gaps in statutory provision. However, individual projects have always had to compete for the same funding, and the current social welfare and housing crisis has sharpened this competition. This has resulted in a marked disparity between resources available to different services, which has impeded dialogue between them.

The grant aid system is geared towards a 'flavour of the month' approach, whereby particular groups of disadvantaged people are spotlighted as 'deserving' at any particular time. This means that voluntary projects often have to prove to funders that the particular group they serve is the victim of greater oppression than others. For day centres, this hierarchy is couched in terms of the visible versus the hidden homeless. Put simply, the visible single homeless are largely white men with experience of the particular institutional circuit or culture associated with homelessness, such as the street, hostel, prison, psychiatric hospital, soup runs and day centres themselves. Most single homelessness research still looks to such institutions for its sample studies. Hidden homeless people are identified as groups who have not shown up in official statistics because they have been systematically discriminated against in the provision of services. For day centres, these include: women; black and ethnic minority groups, gay men and lesbians, and people with disabilities. In some instances, projects have been penalised by funders for taking a broad interpretation of single homelessness. There is, however, simultaneous pressure for projects to demonstrate active implementation of equal opportunities policies.

Compared with that of housing providers, the role of day centres has been largely ignored or underestimated by statutory funders. The Department of Environment's homelessness initiatives have prioritised projects that can be seen to be clearing the streets of visibly homeless people into accommodation. The new 'contract culture' of the community care initiatives largely depends on projects being resourced and geared up to selling care packages which can be seen to be value for money.

Statutory day centres are not generally targeted towards or accessible to single homeless people.[4] A very limited number of probation service day centres nationally operate an open access policy, that is, are not part of the 'punishment in the community' ethos enshrined under Schedule 2 of the 1982 Criminal Justice Act. There are considerable variations in how these are viewed and funded (see chapter 1).

Day centres have an intrinsic relationship with housing provision, particularly in the voluntary sector. Many originated as a daytime complement to night shelters and large direct access hostels operating a curfew, which forced residents on to the streets for large portions of the day (and evening). The movement to close such large institutions and replace them with smaller units of accommodation led many projects to chase the replacement funding made available. It has also left a gap in emergency housing provision. Some day centres expanded into providing housing; others into providing pre- and post-housing support services (resettlement). In some cases, the housing function gradually eclipsed the original non-residential service, largely because bedspaces attract a more secure revenue funding base.

Very few centres originated as the result of a planned and strategic pattern of services, in collaboration with the statutory sector. However, day centres are an important part of the response to homelessness, and share a concern that they will, on the whole, be excluded from current and future planning and funding.

Traditionally, day centres have evolved as hierarchical institutions, rather than as projects organised on a collective or co-operative basis. This has been reinforced by the close connection of the church and associated male hierarchy in their origins. Over 50% of the day centres contacted had connections with the church in some way. Day centre staff have been notoriously underpaid, untrained and powerless in relation to decision making. This clearly has a knock-on effect for user involvement and participation in services.

Centres organised on a collective basis, with staff having equal input into policy and operational decisions, have found that funders will only continue grant aid if they take on a line management structure. Raising money and profiling the organisation are full-time occupations, now undertaken by managers in the scramble for money under the various government homelessness and community care initiatives. The trend towards expansion has profound implications for the development of day centres and particularly for how users are involved in this.

All day centres contacted for this research were founded by concerned individuals/groups of people, or by middle class professionals working in the field. They did not arise as initiatives by single homeless people themselves. This has major implications for the way services have been run: on behalf of homeless people. Once operational, day centres therefore face perennial problems around the nature and extent of user involvement or participation, and there is a pattern of power struggles and different - often hidden - agendas between professional paid staff and their user groups. This distinguishes day centres for single homeless people from other non-residential services, such as community centres and self-help and advocacy models more recently in evidence in the fields of mental health and HIV/AIDS.

Nearly all day centres contacted were in the process of a review of some sort. There was universal reporting of increased numbers and diversity of homeless people seen, especially young people and people with a mental health difficulty. This, combined with growing awareness of the need to offer a range of qualitative support services on a more individual basis, has led many centres to try to streamline their services. Day centres are caught in the dilemma of either continuing to apply a sticking plaster approach to a large number of people, or of making decisions that will adversely affect the lives of some, in order to improve the lives of others.

There is pressure on day centres to be all things to all people at all times, because single homeless people commonly fall through the ever larger holes in the state welfare net. To cope with this crisis, existing day centres are having to review how they deliver services and to whom. Meanwhile, new day centres are being developed in various parts of the country, without the benefit of a shared platform from which to learn from experience. The picture therefore is one of rapid change.

Finally, this report recognises the different problems faced by day centres outside London, where they are often the sole or major resource for single homeless people. Cardiff Action for the Single Homeless and Emmanuel House in Nottingham, for example, are open every day of the year and lack the option to dovetail their opening hours, or to target user groups and services in liaison with other similar local resources. This clearly limits the range and nature of service delivery, with an inevitable pressure to respond generically to most pressing and visible needs.

CHAPTER 1

What is a day centre?
Definitions, historical development and current models

There is great diversity of provision and attitudes in the world of day centres. Consumer choice is, in fact, an important principle cited in the community care legislation.[1] However, centres appeared to exist and operate in isolation, and for many - especially outside London - this was seen as a problem. The reasons for this isolation are various:

- staff do not have time to visit and liaise with each other
- until this report no national co-ordinating or campaigning body had prioritised them
- there has been little sense of an overall common role.

Competition for funding inevitably exacerbates these factors. However, my experience was also that centres did not co-operate because they felt they had nothing in common. This has parallels in the residential sector, where there is a substantial communication gap between people working in large hostels and those in smaller specialist housing services.

Despite differences in language, presentation and ideologies, it emerged that the day centres contacted have more in common than many recognise or have the opportunity to recognise. In aiming towards real consumer choice, common ground as well as difference needs to be more explicitly acknowledged. It is in everyone's interests that the language used should be that which promotes a positive image of user groups, and which most accurately describes aims and services. Similarly, the more day centres know about each other, then the greater the opportunities to learn from each other's experiences, complement services, and offer greater choice to the consumer in reality. The perceived lack of common ground between day centres has created a hierarchy of 'good' and 'bad' practices and services, which has impeded information-sharing and effective networking between services.

This hierarchy often bears little relation to the views and experiences of day centre users. When presented with a choice of centres, such as exists in London, many people were found to be doing the rounds with very precise knowledge of which offered what and when. There was often a particular favourite, *'in the same way you support your local pub'*, as one user put it. Day centres are defined and judged by many of their users primarily on: the price, quality and range of practical services on offer; and on the attitudes of staff, that is, how users feel treated by a worker, volunteer or manager, regardless of whether she is a nun, social worker or community worker. The deciding factor of usage may be as simple as whether a centre provides china crockery and metal cutlery rather than paper and plastic ones, or whether the advice or food on offer is worth the walk or bus fare.

Towards a working definition; common characteristics and core concepts

This section identifies the common ground that can be a starting point towards establishing some sense of cohesion in the development of future services.

It was significant that workers interviewed were better able to define their own project than to address the question of a general definition or common role for day centres. Many emphasised their differences from other services:

'Soup runs are a good pastime for amateurs: we are a professional service responding in a skilled way to a variety of needs' (centre manager).

'Advice centres are based on a straightforward and impersonal exchange of information without support. Here we are offering support with a more holistic approach geared to the whole person' (centre worker).

For many people interviewed, the term 'day centre' carried pejorative connotations. Women in a Salvation Army hostel, for example, immediately associated it with day care, mental health and statutory authorities. More commonly, the term evoked the image of the basic hand-out agency, warehousing a narrow section of the single homelessness population and reminding us that Victorian Britain is not dead.

In order to challenge and redress this stigmatising image, some centres have adopted titles and use language that avoid the terms 'day centre' or 'homeless' altogether - such as 'The Barons Court Project'. Others have deliberately abandoned particular aspects associated with buildings that can quickly become institutional: such as New Horizon, which 'prides itself' on not providing food, laundry or health care surgeries. At the other end of the spectrum, workers in projects such as the Broadway Project and Providence Row Drop-In - which both offer services largely restricted to somewhere to sit and eat - were clear that they were not day centres. The latter were seen positively as offering a more extensive and enabling range of services.

The following are proposed as defining traits to distinguish day centres for single homeless people from other non-residential services such as evening clubs, soup runs or services aimed towards other user groups.

For the purposes of this report:

- **Day centres are geared in part or in full towards single homeless people**. Single people are defined as those without current responsibility for human dependants. The definition of homelessness used by day centres is a broad one and includes: people with past or present experience of sleeping out or of any substandard or temporary accommodation which is not experienced as 'homely'; and people who are housed (often through the day centre) but at risk of homelessness through isolation, harassment, poverty and boredom. Homelessness is seen as a composite state implying, at the least, social and economic dislocation: homelessness therefore does not end at being housed (see also chapter 2).

- **Day centres are non-residential services**, although they may have access to housing or be part of a housing project. Opening hours are varied and usually subject to staffing levels, the existence and opening hours of similar local services, and planning permission. However, day centres are open for at least part of daytime hours and are commonly under pressure from users to extend these to cover evenings and weekends.

- **Day centres share the concept of providing a 'safe', 'warm', 'welcoming', 'culturally sensitive' environment to people who are excluded from mainstream services and amenities**. 'A place of shelter in the face of an uncaring and hostile world' is a characteristic description, which underpins day centres as buildings where homeless people can spend time without having to explain why they need to: 'Without a safe and welcoming environment there can be no beginning' (centre manager).

- **Intrinsic to this concept of 'haven' is that of the 'open door'**. Since services are targeted towards people excluded from other facilities, it follows that day centres operate at least an element of open access: that is, users can drop-in without having to justify their presence, keep an appointment or use their real name. The major intent, even where centres operate a referral procedure (such as the Fanon Project and St. Botolph's) is that entry requirements are kept to a minimum. This presents major operational problems for centres, with wide variations in implementation. Nevertheless, it is still widely used to distinguish services from the more bureaucratised day facilities offered on the whole by the statutory sector.

- **Day centres are characterised by an open ended commitment to seeing people for as long as is needed**, although there are debates about whether this creates an unhelpful dependency. Some centres have adopted ways of contract working with individuals, and appointment systems in addition to the open door. But unless people have been barred for life, day centres generally present themselves as services where it is safe to fail and still to return.

- **In addition to physical daytime shelter, day centres offer a range of practical services geared towards immediate material needs** (referred to throughout the report as basic services). These usually include food and refreshments free or at a low charge; and other facilities such as showers and laundry; luggage storage; chiropody and haircuts; hands-on first aid; use of a telephone; a room to sleep and so on. These practical facilities are usually described as the core service, the foundation point from which users can go

What is a day centre? 13

on to use other services in or outside the centre if appropriate. The core service may also be the end product. Most day centres now see it as the essential beginning for advice and support in other areas: 'we seek as a main outcome referral to other services, but first must come a sense of self-worth' (centre manager).

- **Day centres try to fulfil a social and recreational function** - even if this is as basic as providing a large room with tables and chairs where people can sit and talk. Dependent on money and skills available, most offer more than this: outings, arts and crafts, pool tables and so on. There is sometimes an educational or therapeutic intent behind such activities: such as adult literacy and numeracy classes disguised as quizzes.

- **Day centres now try to provide advice and support, or access to these, on long term needs** centred around housing, health, income, relationships and creative occupation of time. There is variation in the extent to which centres are inward looking or whether and how they try to involve other people in their work. A major debate in the field is whether the provision of on-site services creates a further segregation of homeless people or is a first step towards the outside world. On the whole, though, centres still concentrate the bulk of time and energy on services within the building, and try to meet the whole needs of all their users.

- **The implicit or overtly stated intent of day centres is a holistic one geared to the whole needs of the individual**: 'if you believe that everyone has employment skills, a stable lifestyle, supportive relationships, good health, then day care for adults may seem unnecessary...'[2]

To summarise, for the purposes of this research, a day centre is a front line service geared, in part or full, towards the various needs of single people who have past or present experience of homelessness and who are excluded from other services. Homelessness is a subjective concept and experience. It is not just about where you sleep at night but about whether you feel you have a solid base from which you can lead an independent and fulfilling life. A day centre tries to become that base by providing a range of different services within one building and by treating you with respect and dignity. Provided you keep to minimum rules, you can use the centre as often or as little as you like. You can play cards with your mates, join a job club or get help getting the gas put on in the flat you never thought you would move into.

The main components outlined above define day centres as places that try to be 'home' or 'second home' and 'community' to their users. The essence of the model is an integrated or holistic approach to service delivery: 'rarely defined, much less celebrated' and operating 'within the framework of a comprehensive approach, responding to all other needs such as housing, employment, education and so on, instead of compartmentalising and categorising special needs.'[3]

Day centre models in other fields, such as HIV/AIDS, display similar theoretical characteristics. The Landmark offers a drop-in for social and recreational purposes,

access to a range of advice and services, something to eat and so on. The major differences between such centres and those for single homeless people are:
- their image (see chapter 2)
- the degree of personal and collective power exercised by the user group (see chapter 3)
- the buildings, and the level and quality of resources available, especially from statutory services (see chapter 4).

Understanding the history and evolution of centres goes some way towards explaining why this is the case.

THE HISTORY AND EVOLUTION OF DAY CENTRES
The traditional day centre and its origins

'While the chief object and aim of The Christian Mission is to bring sinners to Jesus, we feel it a duty and a privilege to minister to the bodily wants of the necessitous...Parcels of old clothing, and old boots and shoes will be most gratefully received.' 1870[4]

'We feed, wash and clothe skins...' Whitechapel Mission 1989

Soup kitchens for the destitute were the product of 19th century philanthropy, and pioneered by the Salvation Army in the East End of London from 1867. They were forerunners to the modern day centre. Significantly, Booth and contemporaries heading the Salvation Army soon abandoned the practice of soup kitchens distributing free soup and bread, and expanded their services into food depots, offering meals at a subsidised rate for the relief of the poor. They also quickly expanded into providing night-time shelter and services that would now be described as community support and resettlement.

The 1960s saw both a growth and expansion of the voluntary sector and the re-discovery of the problem of single homelessness. New organisations like the Simon Community aimed to 'hit the headlines all the time with shock reports of sub world horror' and 'dirtied its hands to reach into the gutter'.[5]

Most contemporary traditional day centres have their origins in the 1960s, as a response to the public visibility of 'homeless and rootless' people in a particular locality. The problem was typically identified as groups of middle aged and older white men (hostel dwellers or people sleeping out) without daytime shelter. The impulse to do something about the problem often came from church based individuals or groups concerned to carry out the Christian gospel of succouring the needy and 'reaching out to society's outcasts.' The aim was to 'bring the streets inside' or put a daytime roof over the streets - this being cheaper than providing a night-time roof.

Typically a church crypt or hall would be located, volunteers from the parish enlisted 'to mobilise the community's moral ethics' - involve the local community in responsibility for homeless parishioners - and charitable donations of food and clothes requested. The doors would then be opened to provide a welcome and something to eat for the poor, homeless and friendless in the vicinity. No questions would be asked and no demands made: homeless people were the passive recipients of hand-outs from urban missionaries. The soup kitchen was re-established.

As numbers using the service increased, so did awareness of the range of needs being presented. Day centres still evolve in this way: 'We started as a soup kitchen but people came to us with forms to fill in and other problems and the centre has just developed'.[6] Homeless people would be wanting advice and support, ranging from primary health care to welfare rights and emergency housing on an immediate basis. No other services were interested in providing these and single homeless people - used to receiving no help from other sources - were unlikely to be using these anyway. Typically, a paid worker would be employed to oversee the building, organise the volunteers and fundraise for the extra facilities needed, such as showers, luggage space, a medical room and so on.

The evolution of day centres

Subsequent development depended on a number of factors: resources attracted; the vision/ideology of individuals or of management committees; legislative and funding trends; and regional gaps in provision. Like their housing counterparts in the voluntary sector, day centres were also shaped and influenced by different interpretations of the nature of single homelessness which have developed since the early '60s. These were reactions against public stereotypes of the skid row sub world that were being perpetuated by the media and some voluntary organisations.

An example of factors influencing development is provided by Southwark Day Centre (renamed from St. Giles), which describes itself as the oldest day centre in London. In the project's own words:

'It was established in 1961 to serve the day-care needs of the homeless in the Camberwell area. Initially, it functioned purely as a "soup kitchen", and drew its clientele mainly from the Camberwell Reception Centre. In the 1970s it developed an advice facility, and a welfare rights role serving the same group. The introduction of the Housing (Homeless Persons) Act in 1977 saw a greater emphasis on rehousing emerge, and with the success of our resettlement work, an increase in the provision of post-rehousing support services. Originally the day centre was operated by volunteers, but, in line with current thinking, and in common with other agencies, applications were made successfully to both central and local government, and we now have eight full-time posts.'

Staff are planning to move from the crypt to a new purpose built centre, with a medical focus that reflects funding availability and priorities.

'We are not a daytime doss-house or a daytime night shelter' (centre manager). Most day centre staff now see and define their services as more than or different from the soup kitchen, which has changed into the 'kitchen community' for the

1990s. They try, in various ways, to offer advice and practical support on a whole range of matters but show considerable variation in styles of service delivery.

Examples of development

- St. Botolph's Crypt Centre opened as an alternative to the 'wet' and 'bible thumping' approach of other East End agencies, which appeared to be doing little to change the situation or quality of life of single homeless people. The project adopted a social work model and a dry policy in order to enable individual users to change their situation. The North Lambeth Day Centre similarly reacted against the 'tea and sympathy' approach and advertised itself from the outset as 'a place of change'. Both centres have evolved into complex and growing organisations, offering different services to different groups of homeless people.

- Other day centres evolved as part of a wider organisation, usually providing some sort of housing. New Street (Bristol) originated as a soup run and is now part of a whole range of services from outreach to housing provision and resettlement. It filled a regional gap in the housing market for single homeless people. First Base Day Centre is seen by Brighton Housing Trust as an essential and integral first point of contact for people who would not otherwise have access to the organisation's range of facilities. This model has housing and the prevention of homelessness as the major focus, and is designed to meet the needs of people at different stages of the process involved in finding appropriate housing *and remaining there*.

- Changes in user groups have been a further stimulus to development. New Horizon originated as a non-residential rehabilitative project for drug users, and changed its focus to young people under 21 and its operation to that of a youth centre. Brixton Circle Projects originally operated an evening club for single homeless people (mainly older white men) and this was superseded by the Fanon Project, a day centre for black people diagnosed as mentally ill.

- Although it does not claim to be a day centre, the Broadway Project in Hammersmith and Fulham (an area traditionally dependent on the construction industry and now facing high levels of unemployed homeless people) is located in the same building as the Unemployed Centre. Users often use both services for different reasons, so that they are able to complement each other's scarce resources to offer the main ingredients provided by day centres.

- Emmanuel House in Nottingham provides a further example of development. Rather than expand its own direct service delivery, it has increasingly encouraged links with other agencies to meet the more long term needs of its users. This model is very much building based, with core staff preoccupied with the various aspects of running and policing the premises, and exemplifies the response of day centres to find ways to meet increasingly complex and diverse needs under one roof.

- Most probation day centres are used as part of sentencing: users attend structured programmes for a specified period as an alternative to custody. Those which are open door, and which encourage single homeless users, operate in largely the same way as voluntary sector counterparts but share the prevention of crime as a specific objective. It is argued, for example, that simply providing daytime shelter keeps people off the streets and thereby reduces the chance of arrest as well as offending. The fortunes of such centres appear to have been variable and largely subject to whether the centre could keep up with legislative and organisational changes that have affected the probation service. Minshull Street, Manchester did not receive the staffing levels indicated by internal research findings because the project did not fit in with new evaluation and funding criteria. In contrast, the Wayside Project (Northumbria Probation Service) has been more fully incorporated within mainstream probation work by promoting itself in the language of crime prevention.

The new style day centre

The 1980s not only saw increases in the numbers and range of single homeless people using traditional day centres, but also a more widespread awareness in the voluntary sector of the relationship between homelessness and the structural oppression of particular groups, especially on the grounds of gender, race and culture, sexuality and disability. Equal opportunities was the guiding principle behind the founding of new style day centres such as the Fanon Project and the Deptford Centre.

Such centres were preceded by local research and development by groups of professionals involved in the field and were therefore planned services. They constitute a minority of centres. The open door welcoming ethos was retained, and the need to do something about the public visibility of problem groups was still a founding impetus. However, these new centres started out with the aim of trying to make their services relevant and accessible to other groups in the community who were not visibly homeless, but who were unlikely to approach (amongst other services) the traditional day centres seen as 'daytime doss-houses' for poor white men.

Generally, these centres started out with paid staff recruited on equal opportunities principles; in buildings as ordinary as possible; and with services targeted to the needs of homeless people identified in a particular locality. There was a specific intent to break down the stigma associated with homelessness and a corresponding recognition that traditional day centres were part of this institutional stigma. Just as hostels had been found to create a class of hostel dwellers who became trapped in substandard housing, so day centres created day centres users who appeared to be going nowhere.

The centres therefore originated not only to fill a gap in statutory day care services but also as alternatives to current voluntary sector provision, and with a prime focus on 'empowering homeless people to live resourcefully in the community' (Barons Court Project). Challenging stereotypes and promoting a positive image of single homeless people necessitate advocacy, liaison and campaigning roles, so these centres try to place as much emphasis on the world outside the centre as the running of services within the building. Housing and related advice is usually given high priority, and in some instances (the Southend Centre for the Homeless and the Deptford Centre) these centres have become established as housing advice resources for other agencies as well as for users. Frequently, outside services are invited in to the building to provide services for other community groups and current users, with the aim of breaking down the segregation of homeless people.

Day centres have been commonly compromised by inadequate practical resources, and this applies equally to new style centres. Southend Centre for the Homeless was a planned development following research commissioned by the council into the area's housing needs up until 2003. However, the project has always faced an image problem because its premises have been church buildings. Other centres have a more suitable building without the staffing levels and so on.

There is general recognition by new style day centres that they are only addressing 'the tip of the homelessness iceberg'. Workers in the Barons Court Project rejected the role of distributors of housing and instead liaised closely with the local housing advice centre, in the recognition that their user group is one of many disadvantaged in the housing market.

Most day centres fall somewhere between traditional and new style in a spectrum of evolution. Emmaus House combines the gospel with equal opportunities:

'Some groups attached to churches have real problems about equal opportunities...but unequal opportunities are obvious. The opportunities that people have to get a home are unequal. To address this, an organisation needs a statement, a policy, because goodwill is not enough.'

ROLE AND AIMS

The aim of providing a safe, warm and friendly environment is common to centres, with the term holistic being increasingly used to describe the approach. There was general agreement that centres exist in order to improve the quality of users' lives on some level, with the intent to treat users with dignity and respect. There was further agreement that workers in day centres have to take a flexible approach, and generally be prepared to play a number of different roles - sometimes conflicting - in response to almost any eventuality. 'Sometimes (the role) is arranging a funeral because there is no-one else to do it.'[7] A visit to New Street coincided with the centre playing host to a wedding reception at the couple's request.

The building of relationships between staff and users is critical to services that try to respond to people who are likely to have little trust in other professionals or agencies. In some instances, this befriending role was seen as an end in itself (see Minshull Street, appendix 1). In others, it was the means to the end of equipping users with the self-confidence and information to live ordinary lives in the community.

Having established a safe haven, a flexible approach, and staff/user relationships as a crucial ingredient, day centres varied substantially in how they interpreted and implemented their subsequent role in relation to their users and the outside world. At one end of the spectrum, the London Connection defined one role as 'working in partnership with central government to provide solutions to youth homelessness.'[8] At the other, centres saw their role as little more than holding measures, which stopped some people from dying more quickly than they otherwise would.

Role is often linked to resources available (including local services), the nature and ethos of umbrella organisations (crime prevention or housing provision), as well as historical origins. In addition, the fieldwork identified three major differences in ideological approaches to homelessness, which can be summarised as:

- **containment**: a place of acceptance, with the main emphasis on helping people to survive on a day-to-day basis
- **rehabilitation**: a place of change, with the main emphasis on motivating and enabling individuals to change their life circumstances
- **empowerment**: a place of resource, with the main emphasis on providing people with information, so that they can take control of their lives.

The three models are not mutually exclusive. Many centres take an eclectic approach, which combines a number of characteristics and roles. Pure models are therefore rare, and where examples of individual centres are given below, the intention is to illustrate the main emphasis rather than the total approach. This section is therefore intended as a rough guide to current services rather than a definitive explanation. No one model is presented as 'right': each has advantages and disadvantages, which are briefly explored from the users' perspectives.

The spiritual/missionary approach: a place of containment and acceptance

This model is rooted in Christian philanthropy and this is reflected in the language used. The target user group is usually everyone who is poor and needy, including homeless single people. The main aim is to provide a sanctuary or to create a tolerating community for these people. The approach is non-interventionist and non-therapeutic. Homeless people are accepted for what they are - victims of an unjust world - and the centre or community is first and foremost **'a place of acceptance'**, which bestows dignity by allowing people the right to 'just be'.

The model has an immediate dilemma. Anonymity is respected, which is an aspect preferred by some users. However, homeless people who want further services have to come forward to ask for these, may not know that anything further, such as housing advice, is on offer, or find it difficult to assert their needs. Conversely, staff and volunteers, in providing an accepting sanctuary, are often expected to accept behaviour and attitudes that they may experience as abusive and threatening. The same applies to groups of users, in the absence of mechanisms by which staff can challenge users in ways that do not run counter to the ideals of a sanctuary.

The model is usually hierarchical, with high input from volunteers and various churches. Users are often volunteers themselves involved in running basic services, and many users favoured this over the approach that excluded their involvement on the grounds of exploitation. At its crudest, the role is that of **containment**: homeless people are removed from public visibility for a set period of time in which they can find warmth, food and companionship.

Of the eight project profiles, Emmanuel House would most typify this approach, although it has moved towards a far greater diversity of advice work and liaison with other services (see appendix 1).

Brief summary of users' views

Users were ambivalent about aspects of this model. For example, many appreciated the role played in literally keeping some people alive. The importance of services that catered for immediate material needs was recognised by many people. But it was felt that these centres were not sufficiently pro-active. On the one hand, users directed a lot of criticism against this model as containing homeless people, rather than enabling those who wanted to move on. On the other hand, there were those who argued that day centres should first and foremost address practical material needs and ask no questions nor impose any religious or other value systems in the process. Nobody wanted to be preached at. What also came across strongly was that nobody wanted to be herded in with large numbers of people, especially without safeguards against violent or abusive behaviour.

The social work approach: a place of rehabilitation and change

This model sets out to 'challenge' its homeless user group, as well as the outside world for the 'scandal of homelessness'. The language used is that of groupwork, therapy and equal opportunities. The target user group is people who are 'motivated' to change their circumstances and lifestyle, which often includes their current attitudes and behaviour. This is a condition of using the centre: 'it isn't the place to come for a free meal, it does not see itself as the "great provider" of all things material. What it does offer is a challenge.'[9]

The centre, also a community, is first and foremost **'a place of change'**: homeless people must accept personal responsibility for their lives and behaviour before they can claim their rights. Using services requires a commitment to active participation: attending groups; keeping appointments with an assigned 'key worker'; joining in group discussions and taking on tasks. In order to work with users as individuals who need to change, the model therefore generally has limits on how open the door is. These avoid some of the problems of the spiritual/missionary model, but users often resent curtailment of the drop-in hours or assumptions that they need help and want to change. Staff are not expected to tolerate behaviour experienced as abusive. Conversely, users may feel that challenges to staff are misinterpreted as symptoms of individual pathology.

The model is usually hierarchical, and staffed by 'professionals' comprising a multi-disciplinary team. The role is that of **rehabilitation** of the individual into the community.

The day centre at St. Botolph's comes closest to this model from the sample. As is evident from the project profile, St. Botolph's also offers a number of other services and strategies aimed towards single homeless people (see appendix 1).

Brief summary of users' views

Aspects of this model attracted some of the most vehement criticism, as well as positive praise. Many people valued the greater opportunities for a range of activities and individual attention. However, some users felt that political issues were often obscured by staff as symptoms of personal pathology, with users who challenged parts of the service being labelled demotivated or trouble makers. There were numerous instances of users feeling patronised. One man was reprimanded by a centre manager: 'we must keep the politics out of homelessness.' Asking for a free cup of tea at the end of the benefits week meant listening to advice on money management; not wanting to participate in yet another discussion group on AIDS was not facing up to prejudices and so on. On the other hand, there were opportunities to enter into a dialogue, and many individuals had received valued support in the achievement of personal aims.

In particular, what was critical was whether social workers were seen as genuinely trying to be helpful and offer advice, or whether they were seen as middle class people with little conception or experience of poverty and stigma. As one ex-user said: 'workers make the mistake of assuming that you have personal problems and, then, that they are the best people for you to talk to'. Interestingly, one user interviewed had very different experiences of two similar social work centres. He highly resented being assigned to a keyworker and social worked by one, but valued the structure and individualised support from the other. He felt done to by the one, and listened to by the other.

The community work approach: a place of empowerment and resource

This model sees single homeless people primarily as products of a system based on inequitable access to basic human rights, including education, employment and housing. The language is that of welfare rights and equal opportunities. The target group is usually anyone in the community requiring help and advice on housing and related issues. The main intent is to 'empower' people to take up their rights. Access to information about how the system works is seen as prerequisite towards living ordinary lives in the community: 'The help we are able to give...is very basic. We give information, we give advice, and we give access to resources. We use our knowledge and contacts.'[10] It is the system that needs to be challenged rather than homeless people, who may be experiencing personal problems as a result, not a cause, of their homelessness.

The centre is **'a place of resource'**: users choose their level of participation, but are encouraged towards self-help. The model had tended to be collective rather than hierarchical, with a stress on user involvement. As with the other models, there are some dilemmas and contradictions. Users are often institutionalised into expecting workers to be omnipotent and omniscient, or to stand in queues waiting to be served by workers. Workers may in fact pay more attention to each other's politics than to the more prosaic needs or views of their users. As with the other models, the balance needed to be struck is a fine one, involving some compromises on both sides, and much is dependent on the attitudes of individual workers.

Staff come from a variety of backgrounds but are more likely to be recruited for advice rather than counselling skills. The role is that of **empowerment**, so that users move on to ordinary community and mainstream resources.

Out of the sample eight, the Deptford Centre most typifies this model (see appendix 1).

Brief summary of users' views

This model was most highly rated for access to information and advice, and staff were often praised for taking a non-judgemental approach. People who wanted advice and information did not necessarily want to use other services, such as the social drop-in or food, and the separation of advice from other functions was also advantageous in attracting people who would not otherwise use a day centre.

There were fewer opportunities to remain anonymous and the greater cultural mix in user groups did not suit everyone. Some people preferred the more structured (as distinct from specialist) approach of the social work model. Users generally wanted these centres to provide basic services and to be open for longer hours. Local community services were sometimes criticised for not publicising their services to more people. This was qualified with some anxiety that increased numbers of people would jeopardise their sense of ownership in the project.

CHAPTER 2

Who uses day centres and why?
The experience of the safe haven

Having identified areas of common ground and differences in looking at what a day centre is and tries to be, chapter 2 looks more closely at who uses day centres, with particular reference to the common concept of the safe and welcoming haven.

Important trends

Day centres nationally reported seeing **higher numbers** of people, with dramatic increases over the last decade. Emmanuel House (Nottingham) had seen numbers double in the last five years, to a daily average of 200 people. Emmaus House (Acton) opened in November 1988 and saw eight callers on day one. After three years, the average daily number was 170 people. Bristol's new functional building was already too small to accommodate comfortably the numbers of users and an expanding staff group employed to meet increased demand.

Staff and users also referred to a **greater diversity** in user groups, with particular reference to more young men and women using services (including parents) and more people with mental health difficulties. Day centres were commonly discovering new groups of homeless people, such as young women with children living in bed and breakfast accommodation: 'It's not just the numbers which are a problem - it's the range of people we now see' (centre manager). Many centres were not adequately equipped to respond to these simultaneous trends, which were widely attributed to the economic and political climate of the '80s: 'We are not touching the surface of homelessness. We are not even touching the surface of the 300 who come in here and say they can't stand the streets any more' (worker in traditional centre).

The third reported national trend was increased violence. Workers frequently referred to 'policing the building': 'Every support worker has been hit and abused... the levels of violence were so high at one point that I was frightened to come into work' (centre worker). The day centre environment is a volatile one. The violence seems to go in cycles in individual centres and relates to several factors, but it was a common problem for both users and staff. Users wanted staff to toughen up on their banning policies and to limit numbers. Asked by a worker for opinions on a recent cycle of violence in one centre, a response from users was that it was inevitable when too many people, some drunk, were crowded into a confined space, and that workers should be less liberal in their responses to individuals whose behaviour was abusive or violent.

Second class services?

'Clamp a tramp and tow him to an underground cavern': a wry comment on government policies towards single homeless people.[1]

Is it the role of day centres simply to remove a problem from public visibility? There has been a general assumption that while day centres for single homeless people continue to be overcrowded (as well as underground) they must be fulfilling a valuable role. It is commonly argued that consumers vote with their feet, and therefore those centres seeing the highest number of users must be those that are most successful in meeting their users' needs. There is therefore no need to spend any money on more or improved resources nor to think about why they are needed in the first place.

The equation that high numbers equals success assumes firstly that users have a real choice to exercise. Many users interviewed stated that they used centres out of necessity. Most criticised the lack of choices available, since day centres are few and far between and dominated by traditional style services. The quantity argument assumes secondly that single homeless people are somehow deserving of what the rest of us would experience as substandard or dehumanising facilities. How many people would choose to stand in a long queue waiting for food or a piece of information as a charitable hand-out? Many users of day centres did not regard them as public places, or as places that the public would ever dream of entering:

'They're not exactly on the tourist trail.'

'Marks and Spencer is a public place but you don't expect the police to be forever trawling in there to make arrests.'

It is our daily experience that we feel more at home in surroundings that are physically pleasant, where we can pass time without fear of harassment, where we have some choice over whom we mix with and on what level we wish to participate, and where we feel treated and respected as individuals. This is what most workers wanted to offer.

The minority of centres in a position to limit numbers, separate out functions and groups of people, and look to meet long term needs as well as offer short term solutions, were often criticised as 'political' by funders and as privileged by other centres.

On the whole, day centre staff and their users have been left for so long to get on with it that expectations are very low. This is a trap that is easy to fall into. On countless occasions, workers and users said that they had adjusted their initial expectations and reactions to accommodate the reality that faced them day after day: 'You get used to it' was a common refrain in interviews.

When I visited centres that were not overcrowded or intimidating, where users did praise services in terms of participation, individuality, respect, information and choice, I felt a mixture of profound relief and some initial unease. Enjoying the experience of a women-only day, where workers and users had time and space to get on with what was needed or wanted, I had to question whether lower numbers justified resources. I had become used to large numbers and pressure. Listening to users who had unqualified praise for individual centres, who had felt truly supported and empowered to achieve individual aims, I played devil's advocate to try to prise out the criticisms I had become used to hearing.

But why should services have to justify quality over quantity? There is no doubt that there was a striking difference between users' attitudes towards centres where they felt involved and consulted as individuals, and those where they felt 'treated like cattle' or 'controlled by being lined up in front of a TV'.

For a number of reasons, day centres have found it increasingly difficult to retain an open door to a wide target group and still create an environment experienced as safe and welcoming by individual users. Centres were having to question seriously whether they were achieving their minimum aim of offering a safe haven, when they were having to adopt increased security measures at the door, or having to reduce opening times because of staff sickness or burn-out. Most centres were reluctant to abandon the open door ethos, or to make decisions that would exclude current users. But it would appear from interviews with users that in trying to please everyone, generic centres often please no-one. Many workers were deeply concerned that they were offering 'second class services for second class citizens'.

Bearing in mind that most originated and evolved not as planned services but as responses to gaps in provision, which have simply expanded, many centres are now at crisis point and can often only respond to the most urgent need. All too frequently, users have to 'fight for information' or individual attention, and this depends on who is best able to assert their needs in what amounts to a free-for-all. This situation was commonly experienced by workers and users as frustrating, disempowering and demoralising. Until or unless staff of day centres are able, prepared and supported in refusing to accommodate this process any longer, there is very little hope for their users to be **accepted, enabled or empowered**.

A centre user had this message to workers: *'Historically and to date you have filled the role of "palliative and ameliorative". You should cease to go on being the "bun-bearer" and the "skilly servant".'*[2]

Dry pubs for the poor?

Like pubs, day centres are dominated by men and by a white heterosexual culture that discriminates on all sorts of other levels and reflects the values and power bases of the society we live in. Some pubs/centres are known to be more welcoming to, or dominated by, particular groups - invariably male - or to have a particular ambience or style. Staff and management exercise a lot of control over this by which groups they represent, and by their attitudes and actions. But their customers will also reflect the make-up of the local population, who feels at home with whom, and the perceived quality of the environment and services.

Many people do not use or like pubs/centres because of aspects of the culture or image associated with them. Dependent on many factors, customers walk in knowing or anticipating that there will be other people they do not want to mix with, or who do not want to mix with them. Some expect harassment more than others. There is usually a pecking order of who gets served first or who sits where and with whom. Regulars feel they have more claim on services than newcomers. Anyone new or different can attract attention and feel unwelcome or out of place. Sometimes newcomers - especially noisy young ones - take over and spoil it all. The customers are transient but there is usually a core group of regulars who resist any change unless it means cheaper prices, longer hours and veto over who is allowed in and who gets banned.

There are as many patterns of and reasons for usage as there are individual customers. Some people walk in, take one look and leave; others are waiting for opening time and stay as long as they can. It may be the only place that allows dogs or children. Some people have been banned from everywhere else. It is the social centre for some; somewhere just to eat or drink; a place to meet or make friends or find sexual partners; somewhere to kill or pass time.

There are house rules and behavioural codes imposed by staff and management and exercised at their individual discretion. Staff have the final say: sometimes they are fair, and sometimes not. At the end of the day, customers depend on staff to intervene if they are harassed or abused; staff depend on customers to support them in keeping to ground rules.

Customers like some staff more than others, dependent on the way they feel treated and how efficient staff are. For workers, the hours are often long and the pay is bad; they often know or dread that it will end in tears before closing time; and the management are never around when they are needed. Everyone knows that the real power is in the hands of the brewery.

The analogy ends here. Many people who use day centres cannot afford to use pubs, or would be excluded from them because of widespread discrimination against single homeless people. Alternatively: *'I use day centres when I can't afford to go to a pub'* (centre user).

The welcome

Initial impressions of a service are critical. Some people interviewed had taken one look inside centres and never gone back. This was in marked contrast to how people felt about those centres where workers (or users) welcomed them on entrance, explained what was on offer, and introduced them to other people.

Visiting one day centre for the first time, I entered a fine church building that was spotlessly clean, garlanded with flowers, and empty apart from a couple talking in those hushed tones reserved for places of worship and sanctuary. I was of course in the wrong place. In the absence of a signpost 'Day Centre for Single Homeless People', I spotted and followed the tell-tale empty cans and bottles and a comatose body near a side door. Adjusting to the sudden absence of natural light, I descended into a large crypt packed with people, mainly white men. Most were sitting around tables drinking tea and eating lunch. Some sat on their own; others chatted with varying degrees of animation; a couple of people were muttering vigorously to no-one in particular and were widely shunned by everyone else.

Some young men were playing pool, watched by two bored young women with a baby. There was also some activity around the second hand clothes stall. The worker I had arranged to see was due back at any moment from attending a user's funeral. A harassed looking nun was busy serving up food and asked if I minded going 'to mix with the boys' until he turned up. I could not have lunch because I am vegetarian. The group I sat with made a great fuss to accommodate my awkward request for weak tea, no sugar. One man summed it all up with 'you get used to it, love.' Another said that, much as he appreciated the cheap facilities, 'there must be more to my life than this'.

I visited a wide range of centres, each unique. However, this visit conveys my general impressions of many centres as places that are often experienced as unwelcoming, intimidating, cliquey and depressing. Many users and workers recalled their initial impressions in these ways. A nurse working in a centre outside London described how she had introduced a colleague who had left the place in tears: 'I'd forgotten that I felt like that at first'.

Advice to me from both workers and users included that I should 'dress down' and avoid smart or conspicuous clothes; never let my handbag out of my sight; smoke roll-ups; remove my jewellery; beware the sob story because it was likely to be a con; never get too involved or socialise with users outside work; learn to play pool; and generally be prepared to experience or witness some level of abuse, harassment or violence. I was more armed for discomfort, battle and misery than prepared to enjoy or witness the experience of a safe and welcoming haven.

I was relatively fortunate because of experience as a practitioner. Some day centres, as a strategy, left middle class people to experience first hand the environment. Funders and local councillors were invited to join the lunchtime queue or left to sort out users from workers. This was more damaging when users, especially first time callers, were similarly abandoned and had to find ways to fit in or not, and to find out what services were available.

The exceptions to the general rule were those day centres which had specific policies to ensure that new callers were not simply left to make what sense they could of initial impressions, but were properly informed of what was on offer, including what could be expected of other users and of workers. The Fanon Project operated a formal referral procedure, which included an initial interview with new users: both staff and potential users could then assess whether the project could offer appropriate services. New Street (Bristol) was changing visual displays and information in the foyer reception, to make this more welcoming to black users.

The Deptford Centre employed one consistent person to welcome people at the door, and to introduce them to appropriate services. Employment of a black worker in this role had been found to encourage more black users. All first time callers were asked to fill in one of two forms, dependent on whether they wanted to use the drop-in or needed advice. They were also given a copy of the centre's Charter of Use, which set out what the centre expected of them and what they could expect in return. This made it subsequently much easier to challenge racist, homophobic and sexist behaviour than it was for centres that did not make expectations clear from the outset. A number of leaflets, some translated, were prominently displayed in the reception area.

In contrast, increased security measures in most centres meant that workers were often tied up with 'policing the door', which could include checking breath for alcohol. This role was commonly experienced as demoralising, as well as potentially risky to health and safety in terms of likely responses from users who felt humiliated.

Main reasons for day centre usage

In a discussion group with homeless people they were asked what day centres should and should not do. The first responses were that day centres should provide free or cheap food and should not patronise. This reflected my overall finding that people were often primarily interested in practical services and wanted to be treated with respect.

On the whole, users cited four main reasons for using centres:

- **in order to make out materially**. For people on a low income or no income at all, day centres played a vital role. The practical services appreciated were not restricted to food and tea, but included use of a telephone, sleeping bags, free hair cuts, furniture, showers and towels, free condoms and so on. Some people had nowhere to sleep: the Passage (central London) has a quiet room specially reserved for this purpose. Some centres offered facilities where people could cook their own food.

- **for company and opportunities to socialise**. Loneliness and stigma were powerful themes in interviews. St. Botolph's and Emmanuel House celebrated individual users' birthdays, and were open on Christmas day. Some people used centres as a venue for meeting their friends. People who were housed, for example, often found that neighbours complained about their homeless friends and that it was more acceptable to meet them elsewhere. Some people wanted to make friends or find sexual partners. This was a problem for heterosexual men, who far outnumbered any other group, and was consequently also a problem for women staff, volunteers and users.

- **to break the monotony of a routine**, or to learn ways to occupy time creatively and enhance work prospects. Some users preferred activity to just sitting around. Workers at Minshull Street (Manchester) found that violence was more common in afternoon sessions when lunch had been served and there was nothing further to look forward to. The introduction of activities and varied sessions during that time decreased violence. Outings and holidays were universally appreciated.

- **for information and advice on a range of matters** but predominantly around welfare rights and housing. Some people only used day centres for advice and did not want to use the drop-in. Some centres were beginning to separate out advice from other functions, and to offer appointments as quickly as possible. Legal advice was a popular request from users.

Most people wanted a social environment free from violence and abuse, where they could spend time enjoyably with other people, use a range of good quality and cheap facilities, and have ready access to information and advice. Staff attitudes were a critical determinant of usage. Staff who were appreciated most were those with a friendly disposition and non-judgemental attitudes. Users often appreciated workers who had had first hand experience of unemployment or homelessness.

People wanted to choose how and with whom they occupied their time or used a centre, and a significant number wanted the option of somewhere to socialise without staff around. Frequently, users felt they had to wait too long for workers to spare them a minute, or else that help was forced on them inappropriately or insensitively. Help, it was felt, should be available as and when needed.

Like workers, users expressed opposing ideas about what day centres should provide and who they should be for, and also how much they wanted to be involved in any particular centre. Some people wanted to use the phone, just have something to eat 'and get in and out again as quickly as possible'. Some wanted to remain anonymous. Others wanted to be known as individuals and to play a much greater part in improving the facilities on offer. Some people said they could not survive financially or emotionally without day centres; many wanted to be able to do without them.

Two examples of day centre usage

In order to do justice to the range of views and experiences of users, as well as the diversity of centres, two examples of homeless people interviewed help illustrate this broad spectrum:

Charles had been street homeless for eight years in central London. By street homeless, he meant sleeping out and periodically booking into hostels and bed and breakfast hotels. During this time he used a variety of day centres for: medical care, keeping clean, food, advice on benefits, and company. He stopped using one social work centre because he felt patronised by workers who assumed he needed other help without consulting him: 'they tried to take control.' As a Jewish man, he similarly avoided the worst of the 'magic Christian' centres where you had to pray for your food.

He made a conscious decision when he reached his 40s to 'settle down', booked himself into a hostel knowing it was due for closure and was rehoused within six months. He experienced this move as a difficult one because he felt his neighbours continued to treat him as homeless: 'my face didn't fit.' He continued to frequent all his old haunts, including day centres and soup runs, because he was lonely and without money while his benefits and grants were being sorted out. When he felt more secure, he made more selective use of homelessness agencies.

Wanting 'to make a fresh start and lead an ordinary life' he used local community and mainstream services. He was a member of a local tenants' association, Labour party, library and theatre group; used the community centre and went on their outings; attended local adult education classes; was registered with a GP and solicitor. He knew his local MP personally; and attended AA meetings for his 'controlled alcoholism.'

However he continued to use day centres because this was his most important way of filling in time: 'no other community resource offers me that.' He was a regular at one centre with a strong emphasis on structured activities, and also used this for emergency medical treatment. He used other centres or clubs, 'especially those without any social workers around', in the evenings and weekends mainly for company and sometimes for cheap food. He specifically praised centres where he felt his views were listened to and acted on, and felt that users should have more say in services. However, he felt that most other users were 'too sick or lazy' to want to get involved.

He is an example of someone 'streetwise', familiar with the homelessness scene and ways of surviving, extremely resourceful and with clear ideas on what he could expect from different day centres. He was highly critical of some services, and valued others. Above all, he valued being treated as an individual with views and opinions that he enjoyed discussing.

Colin, a black man in his 30s, became homeless when a relative died and the house he was living in was sold. He could not afford the high rents in the East End and moved south to stay with friends. He had never been in a day centre in his life, but came across a new style centre, which looked to be a place where he could register with a GP: 'I couldn't believe my luck. It turned out to be a centre for single homeless people and I got an appointment about my housing the very next day'. He was particularly impressed by the immediacy of response, the welcome he received and the clarity of information given. He had no objection to filling in forms and giving personal information because he was told why this was needed, and could see practical results as a result of contact with staff.

Although Colin never used the drop-in amenities or any other practical services, he was very positive about the centre as a 'place you can treat like your home'. For him, the centre had been 'an ask your local Thomson'. Unlike the CAB and a black housing association he had been to 'here they help you right up to the last minute.

Other places only help you to a certain extent or lose your file.' He had recommended the centre to friends in housing difficulty.

Whilst continuing to sleep on friends' floors, he kept in touch with the centre about his council housing application and was impressed that staff managed to keep track of his whereabouts and sent regular letters to update him. When interviewed, he was registered with a GP and about to move into a flat through the centre. 'I'm happy with the way I've been treated and would like to help in return in any way that I can.' He felt he would continue to visit periodically after being rehoused, if only for this reason.

This is an example of someone not familiar with street homelessness who would be described as 'hidden homeless'. His usage of centres was restricted to one community resource centre model, and to information and advice around housing and health. His only criticism was that the centre was hidden away.

Most people are somewhere between these examples, but they do illustrate very different experiences, and also challenge common stereotypes both of homeless people and of day centres.

Target user groups

In taking the approach that homelessness is not just about housing, and in offering themselves as surrogate home and community for all in need of these, day centres set themselves a high ideal. Potential target groups are extremely diverse. For example 'all men and women, particularly the homeless, lonely, unemployed and rootless people' (Emmanuel House) or 'all young people aged 16 to 21' (New Horizon). However, people who use day centres represent only a small proportion of the single homeless population, however this is defined. This small proportion still comprises a mixture of people who often have difficulties relating to each other. Day centres that limit numbers, target services for particular groups, and implement clear anti-harassment policies are experienced as safer environments for a wider number of users than centres that do not (see also chapter 3).

Regardless of which ideological model they follow, day centres are products of a society that judges lifestyles according to income, family and housing status. The norm we are still taught to aspire to is that of father bringing home the bacon and mortgage repayments to his wife and 2.2 children. Single homeless people therefore have a negative status and are leading what day centres describe or portray as impoverished, inadequate or stigmatised lives.

Single homelessness implies an absence of those things by which we measure our sense of mental and physical well-being, or which confer status in our society:

- being part of a loving and stable nuclear family unit as sons and daughters and then parents
- being in gainful and useful employment, which enables us to use and develop individual skills, and to be valued and rewarded for these

- having the friends and income with which to enjoy our leisure time and to lead varied and stimulating lives
- enjoying what we individually experience as good physical and mental health, with the education and means to take restorative steps when we experience a breakdown in either
- having the privacy and autonomy to live independent lives, in which we have some control over and say in our immediate environment and circumstances
- having the right to exercise some control or say in the wider society we belong to
- being understood and treated as individuals with a unique contribution to make, regardless of our gender, age, class, race, sexuality, physical or mental status or the lifestyle choices we have subsequently made.

'Homelessness may be a short term problem - rootlessness is a long term depressant.'[3]

For day centres, home does not literally describe a place of bricks and mortar, but is a concept that experientially denotes a more profound sense of attachment, of belonging, of feeling both needed and supported, and of status. 'I feel at home here' commonly conveys subjective feelings of being at ease, of confidence, familiarity and acceptance. Implicit to home is community: day centres describe home as a place where a person feels s/he has the material, psychological and emotional support needed in order to live an ordinary, satisfying and independent life in the community.

The Child Poverty Action Group reported in October 1991 that one in five people in Britain are living in conditions of material poverty. How many of the remaining four fifths would describe themselves as living autonomous, fulfilling and stress-free lives; at the bosom of a caring and supportive nuclear family or community network; in home, workplace and environment of their choice? In these terms, the potential target group of day centres is enormous.

However, most of us have access to one or more of the above components of well-being or status, or have positively exercised some choice over whether to attain them. Day centres are responding to people who often have access to none and who are different from the rest of the population because of poverty of choice or circumstances. The general profile of day centre users confirms them as people who have inequitable access to basic human rights.

The image projected by day centres about themselves and about their users - including language used in publicity and other written material - is critical in determining who uses them.

Image and exclusions

'They've saved many lives but I wish they didn't have to exist' (centre user). Day centres frequently advertise themselves, or are widely viewed, as places of last resort or a 'lifeline for people at the bottom of the pile'. Their literature is permeated with poignant case histories of people leading miserable, disenfranchised, abused and abusive lives: 'So and so had nothing until he started coming here' is the general tone. This is also the most effective or the only way to attract money from statutory funders and charitable appeals to the public conscience. Day centres are mopping up the problems and the people that no-one else wants to deal with, and they stand as an indictment of the indifference of the rest of the world. As one campaign worker put it, day centres are a Cinderella service 'because they are a symbol of our collective failure'. Centres that positively resist this image are also those which attract a more culturally diverse user group, which more accurately reflects the extent and range of the problem of homelessness in the community.

There have been several ramifications of this bottom of the pile image, and of this concentration on users as victims leading highly impoverished lives:

- It serves as a powerful deterrent to large numbers of people who would prefer not to receive services that define or effectively treat them as at the bottom of the heap.
- It has created a general day centre atmosphere that assumes that people who use the service do not do so because they have a contribution to make to it but because they are in need of it.
- It means that walking into many day centres is a statement of negative identity, so that usage in many instances is experienced as a public admission of being needy, or of having failed to lead lives judged according to normative standards of success.
- Workers are often themselves the victims of the same guilt which is used to make the rest of us feel ashamed. This has been called the 'crown of thorns syndrome', which often results in staff, like their users, expecting very little and putting up with a lot.
- The image has a tendency to sustain its own momentum: places of last resort for people with no other choice will continue to attract a majority of people who are used to being stereotyped and treated as outcasts.

Many centre users did not share a view of themselves as needy victims or inadequate, and they were critical of day centres that made them feel either. Referring to standing in a day centre queue, one man explained why he always subsequently arrived much later: *'I've never felt ashamed about being homeless, but there's something so humiliating about the way people stare at you.'* Another user resented the assumptions made by social work staff that he was inadequate because he was single: he did not want parenting, family ties or a monogamous sexual partnership.

Usage of centres was often experienced as taking on a negative self-image or having to be around other people lacking self-esteem or status.

In 1991, a London-wide survey of 531 people sleeping rough, living in hostels and in squats found that 63% never used day centres for single homeless people. Of the remaining 37%, only 9% used day centres daily; 15% weekly; 8% monthly and 5% bi-annually.[4] There is also plenty of experiential evidence to confirm that many people in traditional single homeless groups find alternative ways of spending their daytime hours, or receive the help and support they feel they need from sources other than day centres.

There are a variety of practical reasons for this. For example, many hostels or smaller housing projects provide a range of practical and support services for their residents or tenants during and after their residency. People who are working often (though not invariably) have less need to use centres. But, equally importantly, self image combined with that of a service will be a major factor in determining whether that service is viewed as an accessible and safe environment.

The North Lambeth Day Centre conducted a survey among women living locally on the streets, in squats and bed and breakfast accommodation to find out why they were not using the centre. The overwhelming response was that it was seen as a place for 'dossers' and not for them. The centre has taken many steps to redress this image, and now offers a women-only day that is used and valued by women, despite resistance to this by men.

One young woman interviewed had spent four years living in temporary hostels for the single homeless. She never used a day centre. She had access to other residents and workers for social, recreational, and support purposes. It was only after being rehoused on her own for a while that she sought out the amenities of a day centre: a local rehabilitation centre for disabled people. Homelessness for her had been a circumstance rather than an identity.

Another woman had been new to London and to homelessness when she was 18. The only centre she had used was a community centre combining bookshop and cafe with a safe meeting place for women. Apart from its practical services, this was the only place where she felt safe and accepted as a feminist and a lesbian, by which she primarily identified herself.

These examples confirm the popular image of day centres as traditionally catering for the white street homeless man, with all the associated public stigma. They also confirm the obvious relationship between how an individual sees herself, and what she experiences or perceives as a safe environment.

The prevailing culture

Individual centres reflect to some extent the composition of the local population, and become further known as places welcoming to or dominated by particular groups and cultures. Cricklewood Homeless Concern, for example, estimated that 80% of users were Irish men with a dominant culture based around street drinking. Centres actively select their user groups by their admission criteria (such as a youth centre or project for black people with a mental health diagnosis) and they ban or exclude others on all sorts of levels. However, users will select each other and exclude others by their culture and behaviour. All sorts of variables therefore influence who uses and who feels safe in which centre.

'To understand day centres you have to understand the culture of street homelessness' (centre user).

'When we put a roof over the streets, we also put a roof over the street culture' (centre worker).

One project somewhat ambivalently described an aim as 'having to tolerate behaviour within the centre that would be unacceptable on the streets'.

Describing his experience of street homelessness, George Orwell said: 'it's fatal to look hungry. It makes people want to kick you'; and that the beggar is universally despised because 'he has made the mistake of choosing a trade at which it is impossible to grow rich'[5] (Orwell was not privy to the insights of the modern media). The single homeless man, stereotyped as smelly and shabbily dressed, who sits around parks drinking when he is not disturbing people travelling to and from work, is still widely viewed with fear, suspicion, pity, dislike and above all as someone else's problem. The 'mad bag lady' or 'black nutter' are even more disturbing or terrifying spectres when they surface in public places. The young beggar or prostitute should be at home with parents.

In order to survive in the face of widespread societal discrimination and material poverty, many people using day centres have had to become streetwise. This culture is about learning how to survive materially on a daily basis, and learning how to maintain at least some semblance of self-respect and dignity. Day centres are used as an essential or occasionally useful way of making out; and as places where users do not have to justify their existence. People regarded centres as places for others also down on their luck or lonely: 'At least here no-one looks down on you because you know you're all hard up.'

But nobody wants to feel at the bottom of the heap. People defined and treated in this way often react by creating their own hierarchies. Amongst street drinkers, for example, those who drink meths are the lowest of the low and are often ostracised by other drinkers. The meths drinker might regard himself as better than the junkie. The junkie feels vastly superior to any drunkard. Women who smell, urinate in public, or are loud and abusive are widely disapproved of by their male peers. White people are better than black people. People of different sexualities keep it to themselves. And so on. This is a world where people often cannot afford to be compassionate or tolerant.

Using a day centre is therefore more intimidating for some people than others. The prevalent culture reflects the pecking order, diversity, taboos and prejudices of people who are no different from anyone else except in having to use a day centre.

Most day centres see a narrow section of single homeless people, but this still comprises a wide range of individuals and groups, with attendant problems of competing and conflicting interests, needs and behavioural codes. Day centre staff widely experienced problems in trying to balance competing demands and in combating the prejudices of their users. Services were often dominated by those who could most effectively assert themselves and by those groups which could exercise the most power.

People who use day centres do not share a common identity or worldview except a common distrust of the outside world, and of workers who patronised them. They are difficult, in practice, to **empower** or **enable** because first and foremost they have to survive as individuals placed in a highly competitive setting. They are equally difficult to **accept** for what they are because that means accepting their prejudices and prejudicial behaviour. The three major aims of day centre staff are therefore fraught with difficulties, and the day centre that is a safe haven open to all is a myth.

CHAPTER 3
The holistic approach: community or ghetto?

The safe haven open to all is, in practice, a place that excludes and discriminates, and that is often experienced by workers and users as unsafe, intimidating and disempowering. This safe haven is the stepping stone to community: the vehicle through which users gain the wherewithal to survive, if not flourish, in the community. Chapter 3 examines why this concept presents as many difficulties for centres as that of the safe haven. We look more closely at:
- the concept of community
- issues raised around user participation
- the implications raised by diversity of the user groups.

Day centres take a holistic approach to what they commonly term a 'community' of homeless people. The tendency is to try to meet the whole and diverse needs of this community in one building. Anyone who has lived and worked in hostels or in shared housing for single homeless people will recognise the dilemmas and contradictions involved in forcing people to live together and then calling this a safe place or community.

Centres have increasingly identified two main roles:
- that of creating or facilitating a community of/for users
- that of enabling or empowering their users to live ordinary lives in the wider community.

It is argued by social work and community models that, unless users are given the means to end their homelessness, the creation of a community is a measure of containment rather than empowerment. Participation in the day centre community is therefore a first step towards participation in the wider community.

In fulfilling either or both roles, day centres face common problems of being poorly resourced (see chapter 4); and of finding very little housing or community resources to refer users on to. Acknowledging these major obstacles, the main debate and anxiety in the field is whether day centres are creating ghettos rather than communities. This question informs every other debate around who day centres are for, what they should be doing and how they should be doing it.

It is suggested in the discussion that follows that the concept of a day centre community is a flawed one because:

- community cannot be imposed. Day centre users do not regard themselves as a community of homeless people or behave as such
- user participation in services, fundamental to the concept of community and a stepping stone to the wider community, was not taking place to the satisfaction of most workers and users. Workers held the power and the keys to the building, and users were the recipients of services to a greater or lesser extent

- transience of the user group meant that the regulars were often those who were still dependent on centres and therefore who still felt misplaced in the community
- diversity of homeless people meant enforced social mixing and not community. The only communality between people was a circumstance that most wanted to change, rather than assume as a positive identity. Workers often ended up imposing decisions on and policing rather than empowering their communities.

THE SIGNIFICANCE AND MEANING OF COMMUNITY
Community or ghetto?

A homeless person, now housed, stated that: *'I had to go to prison to get a sense of association and community. Community does not exist for me out here'*. His statement was a powerful reminder that for many people who use day centres, institutions have become community. It raises the immediate dilemma of day centres, that in offering themselves as communities for homeless people (which the three major models do), they may simply be or become part of the institutional circuit that keeps people feeling homeless even when they are housed. How do centres become community for homeless people without also becoming an institution or ghetto?

Recognising this process, some centres were better placed to counter it by offering a more individualised service, and/or by targeting their services towards a broader base of people in the community who are homeless but who have not been through the institutional treadmill. The preventative role of trying to stop people becoming dependent on institutions was of equal importance to that of helping others to break the homelessness cycle. Some such centres have been criticised by funders and other centres as being too 'upmarket' or too specialist for the traditional single homeless groups. They also faced the same problems as other centres in trying to create or facilitate a community for people whose only communality is homelessness.

Which community does a black South American lesbian living in this country belong to? What sort of community centre would she feel at home in? She is 27 years old and sleeping on friends' floors. Is her community a day centre for homeless people? What would she expect of it?

One day centre may call itself a community; others may regard it as a ghetto. Its users are likely to have similar mixed views. Community is a term that is used frequently but rarely defined in the context it is used. It means different things to different people, according to individual experience and political perspective. However, when people refer to community it means something desirable; ghetto is used to imply something undesirable. Community is participation and empowerment, a positive recognition of communality and a shared goal to shape the world, so that it is responsive to individual and collective need. Ghetto implies a defensive reaction to a stigmatised identity that is imposed by the rest of the world. Community is choice. Ghetto is imposed. Community develops and changes. Ghetto encloses and retreats.

Community centre: a fantasy?

The philosophy of many day centres is rooted in Victorian Christian values, and a wide range of denominations are involved in providing services to single homeless people. These values present an ideal of family and community that is at odds with contemporary reality. As one user pointed out, Christ himself was a single homeless man whose lifestyle could be seen as far from conventional. He would surely have been unhappy that the myths about family and community are most evident at Christmas time, when the media inevitably includes copy on the plight of street homeless people. Christmas serves as a reminder of the ideal community in which we do not live, and of the narrow interpretations that restrict our choices as people.

Bearing in mind Christian roots, along with the other perspectives in the field, the following is offered as the ideal of community:

A body of people who recognise a natural connection, a positive common identity, who take control of their lives and environment by acting co-operatively to achieve shared goals that are mutually beneficial. A community centre is a building that serves the varying needs of that body of people. Once again we see the principles on which such a community could be based: individuality, participation, respect, choice and information.

Imagine having a building, a community centre, just round the corner, where you could pop in any time for just about anything you need or feel like. From a sauna to a holiday. There is not only a GP but a homoeopath and whatever else keeps you sane and healthy. No excuse for putting off keeping fit if you want to, with all those facilities. You get the chance to learn and to do all those things you wanted to but never had the time, money or energy for. And there are opportunities to travel without joining the armed forces.

There are like-minded people and others whom you enjoy meeting when you call in. You do not have to hang on to a label and stick to others wearing the same badge. You can be yourself and that can change because you are learning all the time from other people and they are learning from you. And there are always people who are around just when you need that bit of advice about the poll tax summons, or you want a heart-to-heart about relationships and life in general.

No-one is in charge and no-one is at the bottom. You can influence what happens in that building, and what is happening locally and much further afield because your views count on every level. And it is all free or very cheap for those without money and subsidised by those with money.

This fantasy community centre is very different from the dry pub analogy, but comes closer to what day centres aim for.

There are many reasons why it is unrealistic to expect to find everything and everyone we need in a building that is big enough to be multi-functional and small enough to make us feel at home. Most of us do not need such a building, since we have access to a whole range of services and amenities which meet our needs, from advice and information through to socialising and recreation. Moreover, we do not live in a political and economic climate that encourages people to live co-operatively.

That does not mean to say we dismiss the fantasy as totally unachievable or ludicrous. A fantasy can be a blueprint for reality and vice versa. This one simply translates a common wish for a good quality of life into one building, and into an enjoyable experience.

The fact that such a community centre reads like the science fiction of the '90s is comment on the values imposed by the haves upon the have-nots and the increasing gap between the two.

Community centre for homeless people?

Imagine how much more fantastic is the concept of a community centre for single homeless people. If day centres were really centres that evolved and were shaped as grassroots communities, they would be a powerful lobby and not a marginalised service. This is not simply the result of poor resources. You have only to visit London Lighthouse[1] and then a crypt centre to see the different effects of self-help and lobbying, and charitable hand-outs.

Single homeless people who use day centres are not a body of people who recognise a positive common identity, and then take control and action to achieve shared goals. All sorts of people become homeless for all sorts of reasons, and the problems they face are about access to housing and to community resources. Homeless people spend time with each other because they have to in order to get access to housing and community, or because they have no other choice. Some homeless people may argue for the right to lead alternative lifestyles, but want an end to homelessness. When single homeless people only feel at home with each other, is that choice or imposed?

When people get together, call themselves a community, take control and act together to make changes, it can be threatening to other people who have a vested interest in things remaining the same. Day centre staff rely on the existence of homelessness for their own living, and some were clear that their ultimate aim of ending homelessness would mean the closure of their projects and the loss of their incomes. However, some earned more than others, or belonged to organisations that expanded at another organisation's cost. Others were prepared to struggle along asking for nothing but thanks, which frankly users often had no reason to give. A more happy balance was struck by those centres where workers acknowledged their power and used this to enhance that of users. Such centres were outward-looking services, which gave equal priority to work outside and within the building.

There were exceptions to this, but, on the whole, the people with the power, the staff, were as threatened by the prospect of user collective action as councils are by tenants associations that function, and governments are by local authorities that are 'militant'. An example of this in action was the description of a discussion group that turned into an analysis of homelessness in the context of government policy. At the end of the group, users were told by staff that they were using politics to hide their personal problems. An emergency staff meeting was called in response to this. The person describing this incident was clear that workers were threatened by the idea of users identifying homelessness as a political issue, and perhaps questioning what workers were doing about it.

To make a direct comparison, people with HIV are not a natural community. Day centres in this field similarly experience difficulties in providing equal services for different groups of people in need, and in ensuring that their services are responsive to and representative of the different needs presented. However, gay men with HIV recognised communality in the discrimination they faced, saw this as a political issue and were not prepared to accept second rate services in which they had no say. Persistent campaigning and public education by the people affected has meant that centres for people with HIV/AIDS are far better resourced and offer a greater range of services than most day centres in the single homelessness field. The Landmark, a small local centre, does offer a range of allopathic and alternative health services, and this is not considered fantastic or a waste of money.

The only communality between single homeless people is a circumstance that most wish to change, with the option to select from a choice of services that will help them to that end. Unless day centres can equip people with the information and the means to end their homelessness, they are imposing a concept of community that is in reality a ghetto. The trend in some centres towards outreach and resettlement work is acknowledgement of the importance of concentrating at least as much effort outside the building, in order to break down the discrimination that makes and keeps people homeless. However, campaigning and raising public awareness were, for various reasons, roles that centres were unable or unwilling to take on effectively.

USER PARTICIPATION OR EMPOWERMENT

Assuming that the role of day centres is not to create ghettos but to enable their users to have a place and a say in the community of their choice, there are two main questions facing centres:

- how to ensure that services are responsive to what users need, rather than what workers feel they need or can provide?
- how to equip individuals to live resourcefully in the community?

It is frequently argued that, by participating in the day centre community, users will gain the confidence, skills and information with which - at least - to cope with the pressures of the modern community. This was particularly true of people with experience of institutions and therefore accustomed and expecting to be controlled and directed by staff. The starting point for centres was finding the time and creating the structures to ensure that users had a say in the services set up for them.

An interesting initial comparison to make is the clubhouse model, which originated in the United States as a reaction against the standard and institutional provision of day care to people leaving psychiatric institutions. The model is a membership based one, in which users have some control and say over their own intake. Staff do not hold separate and closed meetings. *'The single most significant way that..we can provide rehabilitation for a member is for him (sic) to experience being needed.'*[2] Centres and services are created and designed so that they cannot function without member participation and involvement: *'Clubhouse staff are sufficient in numbers to engage the membership, yet small enough in numbers to make carrying out their responsibilities impossible without major member involvement.'* To function, both staff and users have to unlearn years of patterned responses and roles: staff have to learn how to give up power and users how to take it.

This is not to suggest that day centres should cut their staffing levels. But most centres were inadequately staffed, while many users wanted to contribute their skills. Some centres, like the Fanon Project and the Deptford Centre, compensated creatively for staffing shortages by asking users to take over aspects of their work, such as visiting in hospital, showing new users around the building and so on. Self-help became a reality for some users, who went on to form supportive relationships or networks outside the centre, and project staff felt they had learned valuable lessons from this. Both had significantly fewer problems with violence than other centres.

The voice of users

Far from describing an extravagant fantasy, users often had very modest and reasonable expectations of an ideal day centre. What people wanted from services may have been more basic than workers often acknowledged. Many people wanted somewhere to socialise in an ordinary and pleasant setting, without workers around. Users commonly wanted social activity in the evenings and weekends. Users did not have access to buildings without the presence of workers. Neither had many found alternative venues. Workers wanted users to take more responsibility, but were not always prepared (or supported in) taking the risks or steps this would entail: such as allowing users unsupervised space in which to meet, or helping them to set up their own offshoot social clubs.

Users who felt positive about the service simply wanted more resources or worker time to be available. With some exceptions, people who expressed a lot of criticism were content to tinker around with minor changes rather than make the wholesale sweep that their feelings seemed to justify. Young people had far higher expectations and went much further towards describing the fantasy community centre. Expectations reflected the extent to which people were used to being listened to and having their views taken seriously. This further reflected the degree to which people were accustomed to depending on institutions.

Users were most positive about individual centres or staff members when they felt their views had been listened to, where they felt treated as equal and individual human beings, when they had received a helpful individualised service. Commonly, centre staff felt that they did not have the time or means to hear their users. Many staff themselves felt their views were not heard, or did not count, in their respective organisations.

'Although the ideal situation is one where services are tailored to priorities identified by homeless people themselves, the reality is somewhat different. Pragmatic considerations determine otherwise.'
(centre report: social work model).

'I know we should consult our users far more than we do, but we simply don't have the time even to sit down with individuals and listen.'
(centre worker: spiritual missionary model).

'In practice, user participation means nothing. Users either don't want to attend meetings, or else they ask the same old things like why is there a women-only group?' (centre worker: community model).

'Only about 20% of my time is spent in clinical diagnosis. The rest is spent just listening to people as individuals'
(community psychiatric nurse working in centre).

Workers who had the time often felt that speaking with people individually was a more effective way of hearing views than the standard user/staff meeting. User involvement with services starts when that person enters the building and ends when s/he no longer wants or needs to use the service. That process could be completed in one visit or over several years. Those projects that recognised this as a process organised their services so that first time users knew what was on offer, could discuss how they wanted to use the centre and were aware of any conditions or expectations of centre usage, such as anti-discriminatory policies.

Unless users felt involved or that they had some power to exercise, they were unlikely to attend the formal mechanisms that staff set up for their voice. User representation at decision-making level was generally recognised as tokenistic, especially in hierarchies where workers themselves were removed from decision-making and, in turn, handed down decisions to users. Moreover, users could not be expected to participate in decisions about project funding or equal opportunities, if they were not familiar with the jargon and values used. A further reason why no centre claimed 'to have got user participation right' is that users got fed up with attending meetings or discussion groups because nothing seemed to happen as a result of these. This is not unlike the low public response rate to elections: what is the point of voting unless you believe it will make a difference?

Them and us:
the conflicts between staff and users

Users had different priorities from workers, reflecting major differences in culture, class and power between the two groups. Meetings between the two - often the main or sole mechanism for user participation - were characterised by user requests for more and improved practical services on the one hand. On the other, workers usually said no because of budgetary constraints, or because their job descriptions or value systems dictated different priorities.

Users resented having to mix with each other because staff told them that they should be tolerant. One man described how a worker made him go back and sit next to a woman 'who was not only mad as a hatter but who also stank'. This was for him a supreme insult: clean and tidy appearance was essential to his self-respect and, in his terms, he was being required to compromise that.

Help or support was experienced by users as conditional; and there were major problems between young middle class staff groups recruited on equal opportunities lines and older streetwise users who resented being told how to think or behave. One user, referring to the power of day centre workers, contrasted with the disenfranchisement of their users, posed the question *'What is more important - the political or religious orthodoxy of workers or the views of the users?'*

Users and workers were trapped in perpetuating some classic features of the closed institution. Where staff tried to upgrade services by providing a choice of healthy or culturally diverse food, users wanted to stick with the 'stodge and chips' they were used to. Where users wanted a more pleasant or safe environment, staff felt they would not feel at home or that they would ruin Habitat furniture and graffiti clean paintwork.

Workers tried hard to redress their image problem, commonly by improving accessibility to women and particular ethnic groups. Some users frustrated this with their racist and sexist attitudes or behaviour. But challenging or excluding current users effectively meant punishing or judging people who were themselves powerless. Users, in turn, felt patronised or preached at by workers, and there was some cynicism that saying the right things got rewarded by brownie points towards resources. Young people were said to be more effective at playing the system than older users.

Workers generally wanted users to be more involved in the running of services, or at least consulted more than they were. But they would then refuse to put locks on toilets because users were untrustworthy and would drink or fix in them. Workers asked users what they wanted, and would then say that playing darts was too dangerous. And so on.

A classic example of this stalemate position is recorded in the minutes of staff/user meetings in one centre, where barring and rules emerged as issues at each meeting. Users wanted the rules discussed, clarified and displayed on the walls. People would then know clearly what was expected. Staff resisted this on the grounds that it would be unwelcoming and institutional. The same centre had a sign conspicuously displayed on the external wall banning the use of pills and syringes, despite complaints from users that this made them feel stigmatised.

Creative involvement

The following are examples of different ways in which users felt involved in services:

Campaigning

One user interviewed on an initial visit to a day centre was extremely critical of services on offer, of staff attitudes and of other users. Her feelings changed significantly when she was invited to participate with staff in playing a role outside the centre, to raise public awareness around homelessness: 'I've really got into this thing about homelessness as a political issue'. She subsequently took a much more active and helpful part within the centre, including representing the views of other users at meetings.

There were several instances where users wanted to campaign on an issue - such as the overnight closure of public toilets - and were discouraged from doing so, largely because this might upset funders. If homeless people are to change their situation, they have to challenge the discrimination that faces them every day. Unless day centre users can recognise their only communality, they will continue to have problems in being required to tolerate each other.

Consultation

A study conducted in 1979 incorporated the concepts that women users had of an ideal day centre and their practical suggestions around design of a new one.[3] Subsequent evaluation found 'high satisfaction rates with the new building'.

Users cannot be expected to take an interest in their environment unless they are involved in decisions affecting it. Workers cannot evaluate and develop their services without feedback from users. New Street (Bristol) undertakes an annual survey, which both monitors who uses the centre and their views on services. Some projects used meetings to discuss specific topics or current issues, such as whether a centre is suitable for children, before reaching a decision. Some centres had found that any new development needed the understanding and consent of current users. Introducing a new service for drug users was likely to cause a mixed and hostile reaction without previous dialogue.

Contributing skills

Older regular users of traditional centres often recalled the 'good old days' when things were run on a shoestring budget and a volunteer workforce - not because they preferred the services offered then, but because they had felt more needed in the running of the centre. Some users pointed out that if they were left to get on with running clothes stores and preparing food, paid staff could concentrate on advice work and training. If they could fix the shower or build a wheelchair ramp, why should centres have to spend money on outside contractors?

Workers were divided on whether this was exploitation, reinforcement of the trusty system of institutions, rehabilitation, or simply healthy involvement. There was an element of each in different centres, according to their general style and other ways in which users were involved. Users did not feel patronised, exploited or fobbed off by centres which paid them a going rate for pieces of work, or where they had contributed their skills and energy because they wanted to.

Mutual support/advice and information

Thames Reach Housing Association facilitated a drop-in for people at various stages of being housed, for the exchange of information and experience.[4] One result was the production of a practical handbook for use by anyone going through a similar process. Some day centre users had a better working knowledge of, for example, the benefits system than workers and were more than happy to pass this on in advice workshops.

There is a potential role for users to visit and liaise with local community resources and to share that information. This would make it far easier for people to start using and exploring services previously inaccessible or intimidating. Workers would also have first hand information on resources and could make confident referrals.

These are very basic examples of a few ways in which workers and users found they could co-operate in the shared goal of ending homelessness and improving quality of life. Any more grandiose claims at empowering homeless people would require a restructuring of services, so that power really did shift from professional hierarchies to user groups.

Taking responsibility, or letting go of it, requires risks, commitment and changing patterns of thinking and behaviour. Current structures reinforce the power of service providers rather than service users. There is a climate of fear when it comes to challenging the system that produces this, especially when money is involved. Funders are not generally prepared to back risky ventures, and a network of small scale co-operatives would be riskier than isolated monoliths competing with each other.

DIVERSITY OF USER GROUPS: POSITIVE MIX?

On the grounds that their users have often lived a public and/or institutional lifestyle and may want to remain anonymous, many centres do not keep detailed or accurate records. These are often restricted to crude head counts or take-up of meals. More detailed breakdowns vary according to such factors as:

- funding criteria and expectations
- the need for particular information to highlight a local gap in provision
- the project's level of awareness of particular issues.

The data collected by centres is therefore patchy, often impressionistic and can be misleading. For example, one worker estimated that 90% of users were probably HIV positive 'because of the lifestyle they lead', reflecting that worker's assumptions rather than an informed statement.

However, some general trends did emerge, which also indicated the diversity and difficulties among user groups and the difficulties for workers. Although some day centre populations were more diverse than others, most centres experienced problems between different groups of current users, and in trying to respond appropriately to these differences.

Equal opportunities

Gender

'Where ignorance prevails, vulgarity exerts itself' (woman centre user about men centre users).

All day centres contacted were dominated by men. On the whole, women comprised less that 20% of the total user group. Most centres reported increased numbers of women over the last decade. In particular, there was a trend towards increased numbers of women aged under 25, with sexual abuse often cited as a reason for homelessness. Concern was expressed by many centre staff about the numbers of young women who were pregnant or with small children, whose experience of mainstream health and social services had often been negative. Most workers did not feel that their services were suitable for children, in terms of physical environment and support levels, but in some instances did not exclude them because their mothers had nowhere else to go.

In celebrating International Women's Day, New Street had uncovered a new area of need, presented by mothers living with children in bed and breakfast accommodation. Staff took the view that it was more appropriate to lobby for resources to be made available to this group by the statutory sector than to try to meet this need themselves.

Youth centres, such as New Horizon and the London Connection, saw a higher total proportion of women, including black women. Centres offering advice services separate from drop-in amenities, such as St. Botolph's and the Deptford Centre, also tended to see higher numbers of women from a variety of backgrounds.

Nationally, many centres were beginning to target services to meet the needs of women, usually by a women-only session. Take-up of these was often disappointing. Women interviewed were often under peer pressure to conform to the dominant norms, as well as to be seen to be treated no differently by middle class workers. A regular centre user who attended women-only sessions complained that 'they're trying to make me ladylike.' She felt that she was being required to change the only ways she knew to survive in a man's world, and experienced the language and attitudes of some workers as a value judgement on her. Nevertheless, she needed the women-only space. Young women interviewed at North Lambeth's women-only day initially described it as a waste of time. They went on to comment that when the men were around they never got to use the facilities, and that it was much better being able to do what they wanted, rather take a back seat to their partners.

Such examples suggest that women may often feel diffident about claiming space; suppress important parts of their experience or identity; or regard well intentioned attempts to empower them as patronising or threatening. Women may not be enthusiastic about changes that mark them out as different, but the general experience was that, once initiated, such changes were often appreciated on some level. After initial suspicion or resistance, for example, women-only sessions often provided the first opportunities to raise basic issues such as the need for separate toilets (with locks) and the need for free sanitary towels as well as razors.

St. Botolph's wanted to provide a separate entrance for women, so that they did not have to run the gauntlet of men on first arrival, but women users rejected this because they wanted to be treated equally. As an alternative, workers liaised with other services to organise a network of meeting places for women. Swansea, on the other hand, went ahead with a second entrance and found this did attract more women. Projects reported that it took a long time to establish space for women, required commitment from the whole staff team and management, and that men users often reacted by wanting their own group.

Women users and staff frequently experienced harassment from male users and dealt with it in varying ways. Older women often sat on their own, or did not stay long. 'Streetwise' women had often learnt to give as good as they got and were better able to survive in this setting than women new to the scene. Many young women only attended with their male partners.

Many women workers and volunteers put up with all sorts of pressures: *'how can I tell someone who reminds me of my grandfather that he is sexist?'* Some felt they could not rely on their male colleagues for support: *'I had to stand back powerless while a man shouted at a woman that he wanted to rape her because I knew I'd get no back-up.'*

One male worker interviewed commented that sexism could only be challenged 'if workers speak the same language as users' and recognised factors like class and culture. When his female colleague explained at a users' meetings in very plain language how it felt to be manhandled and chatted up, and why women did not return for a second visit, users started to react very differently, showing much greater respect and challenging each other's sexism. How users experienced challenges to their attitudes or behaviour rested largely on who did this and how. *'Challenging people does not mean writing people off. If workers need training in equal opportunities, so do users'* (centre worker).

Ethnicity

All centres were predominantly the domain of white British people - with the obvious exception of the Fanon Project. On the whole, white British people comprised more than 90% of the total user group. Although black people are disproportionately over-represented in institutions such as prison and psychiatric hospital, they are under-represented in most day centre services. Again, youth centres and advice services tended to attract higher proportions of different ethnic groups.

Many centres reported that at least significant numbers of their users were of Irish or Scottish descent. A few projects saw a handful of Asian homeless men. Asian women were conspicuous by their absence. Anecdotally, an Asian worker was told at the door of one centre that it 'wasn't a place for people like her.' A limited number of centres offered separate groups for people of different ethnic origins, which tended to be even more sparsely attended than sessions for women. As with gender, specialist services for one group often resulted in another group wanting something similar. One centre that celebrated St. Patrick's Day then faced requests to celebrate St. George's Day.

Interviews with black users of the Fanon Project confirmed the importance of a specialist service that was safe, at least for black Caribbean men. Having the triple stigmatic labels of mental illness, homelessness and being black, users of this centre regarded it as an oasis in an institutionally racist world. Black men on the streets were even more likely than their white counterparts to be picked up by the police, diagnosed, sectioned as mentally ill, and excluded by mainstream and other voluntary sector services. The Fanon Project saw its role as providing a culturally sensitive environment and as challenging the system that discriminated against its users. Advocacy at mental health tribunals or police stations, and liaison with other services, were as important as initial interviews with all new users and providing a Caribbean meal.

Only exceptionally did any centre offer translation services or access to these. Most staff and volunteer groups were mainly white. Centres that employed people of different ethnic origins found that this made a difference to the composition of users' groups.

Sexuality

'Three lesbians, one bisexual and the rest are still making up their minds.' This was the description of the staffing composition in one of the few projects that had seriously begun to address sexuality and discrimination.

Most day centres did not monitor user or staff/management groups in terms of different sexualities, but were clearly dominated by a heterosexual culture. Very few centres offered specialist or sensitive services for gay men, lesbians and bisexuals or even acknowledged their existence. Workers tended to be more aware of gay men than of lesbians, and often kept this confidential from other users or staff because of anticipated discrimination.

'It makes you very introvert being with men all the time. You just can't talk to them about anything meaningful' commented a lesbian centre user who also described herself as a feminist. In the absence of dialogue and supportive structures, it was impossible for staff and users to be honest about their sexuality. One young woman had to be very assertive, in order to face the usual judgements and prejudices when she came out as a lesbian by openly attending a lesbian/gay group. More commonly, users and workers who felt safe to come out in interview were terrified if this became known in the centre. Lesbian workers left projects because they were unsupported and could not in turn offer support to hidden lesbian or bisexual users. Homophobia emerged as one of the most hidden but disturbing aspects of the average day centre environment.

Centre staff placed a lot of emphasis on the importance of personal relationships, and then coyly refused to acknowledge sexuality as an important issue. As one user commented: *'it's alright for staff to have sexual relationships, but homeless people have no right to think about it!'* Issues around celibacy, safe sex, and different orientation were as important to homeless people as any other cross section of the population.

Age

All day centres reported seeing increased numbers of young homeless people under 25, and this was widely attributed to changes in benefit regulations particularly affecting this age group. Some centres, such as in Bristol and Swansea, noted seasonal variations in age groups: for example, more young travellers had started to use their services in the summer months. Other centres, like the Passage in London, had had to ban young people under 25 because they were coming to dominate demands on their services. This steady upwards trend in numbers was felt by users and staff to be one of the most significant changes in day centre usage over the last decade.

There appeared to be a disproportionately high number of young people with experience of local authority care. New Horizon found that 40% of their users had been in care. 37% of Bristol's sample survey (all age groups) had been. Anecdotally, many young users in turn had children in care, or were at risk of such proceedings being taken. There was reported widespread suspicion among young people of statutory authorities, and centre workers frequently commented on the dearth of resources to refer young people to. Where it was mentioned, it was hoped that the Children Act would result in increased accessibility of mainstream services to young people.

Day centres widely experienced problems in the enforced mixing of age groups: 'they're full of old men who sit around like cardboard cut-outs' or 'can't you do something about these youngsters? They're rude, noisy and aggressive.' Emmanuel House was typical of such problems: the main social area was dominated by young people occupying the central space, with older people dispersed around the periphery.

Most people felt that there should be separate facilities for people under 25, or at least separation by space and services offered. Emmanuel House had undertaken a feasibility study, which incorporated the views of young homeless people, into the development of a separate centre for people under 25.

Mental health

'I've been diagnosed schizophrenic, but what does that mean? What is mental health anyway?' (centre user).

Centre workers generally commented on the increased numbers of people with a mental health problem using their services. Estimates ranged from 5-70% of the total user group, and averaged at around 30-40%. Increased numbers of users with a mental health difficulty was commonly linked with the movement to close down large psychiatric hospitals. However, there appeared to be increased awareness of mental health as a result of the community care initiatives. It is therefore a matter of speculation as to whether centres were seeing increased numbers of people, or were simply more aware of mental health as an issue and were also widening their definitions to include groups and individuals previously categorised differently (for example, people with an alcohol or drug-related problem).

This whole area was fraught with definitional difficulties and staff typically felt that they were insufficiently qualified or trained to respond appropriately. Workers often recognised or stressed the psychological stress of homelessness and had always been familiar with users experiencing or exhibiting situational mental distress. But, on the whole, it was not clear to workers how to distinguish between this, formal medical diagnoses and different levels of experience of psychiatric services, and self-definitions that were as vague as feelings of depression or anxiety. A further problem was that workers may have labelled behaviour which they experienced as problematic as a symptom of individual pathology, whereas those individual users felt that it was perfectly rational in the circumstances.

In this confusion, it may therefore be inaccurate or misleading to assume that more people with a mental health difficulty directly correlates with the closure of hospitals. The Joint Forum on Mental Health and Homelessness[5] would argue that the problem for homeless people is as likely to be that of discharge from acute beds on to the streets or into inadequate accommodation as discharge from long-stay beds, and that there is a causal relationship between homelessness and mental distress.

Regardless of definitional problems, centre users and workers commonly referred to mental health as an important issue, and users who were visibly disturbed or behaviourally 'different' were often left alone. Some centres acknowledged that the environment was hostile to anyone conspicuously in mental distress and preferred to refer on such people as a matter of course. More commonly, centres were making use of such services as community psychiatric nurses and were critical of the lack of support available to most people in the community.

Day centres operating a social work model were most likely to offer formal counselling. Most other workers felt that all they could offer was a 'listening ear' or - where available - referral on to a more appropriate service. Day centres generally lacked private interviewing space, which placed obvious restrictions on the nature of responses to individual needs. But on more than one occasion I was aware of people being 'counselled' on sensitive topics, such as sexual abuse, in public areas.

Physical health

Significant numbers of people were estimated or known to be in need of medical attention. Physical health problems cited were wide-ranging, from immediate first aid through to hospital admission. Day centres typically provided access to primary health care facilities via walk-in GP and community nurse surgeries, and were increasingly providing other health services such as needle exchanges, health education sessions around basic diet, HIV/AIDS, alcohol and drugs and so on. As in other areas, the experience of staff was that users did not have equitable access to mainstream services and often would not use these because of previous negative experiences.

Most centres were not able to cater for people using wheelchairs because of the design or location of the building. However, many users were in receipt of or entitled to sickness or disability benefits, and experienced different degrees of mobility problems associated with poor living conditions. Southwark Day Centre found that over 60% of their sample users defined themselves as having a mobility problem.

In this area, as in many others, people using day centres were those who should have had a statutory right to housing and to community support services.

Income and employment

The vast majority of people using day centres were unemployed and subsisting on a low income or no income at all. From users' perspectives, the importance of day centres as material providers should not be underestimated. On the whole, few users defined themselves or were defined as professional, but many had skills that were underutilised. Whilst often encouraging users towards employment, many centre staff felt that this was a hopeless task in the face of widespread unemployment, exacerbated by the economic recession. Centres commonly geared their programmes or services towards access to training, or the creative use of time.

Users of New Horizon had access to a Job Bus - a mobile service staffed by people sympathetic to the particular difficulties that young homeless people face in finding employment. The Deptford Centre was working with the Industrial Society to find ways of working with local employers to break down their discrimination against homeless people.

Prison and offending

Day centres frequently referred to significant proportions of their users groups as having had some contact with the criminal justice system, from arrest to imprisonment. It was widely agreed that users were often vulnerable to arrest or offending because of their lifestyle and economic circumstances. Probation-run centres felt they were playing a preventative role, simply by providing somewhere off the streets with cheap or free amenities. Many users had had some contact with the probation service, if only for hand-outs. By working with the probation service, centres had a role to play in ensuring that the cycle of arrest, imprisonment and homelessness was acknowledged as a serious issue.

Housing situation

'For those of us who chip away at the "coal face" of single homelessness, we can only begin to see the stars/sky/sunlight when there is an obvious statistical upturn in that elusive product labelled "affordable housing".' [6]

All day centres contacted saw a mixture of people who were: literally without shelter; in a mixture of temporary or insecure accommodation ranging from hostels to friends' floors; and those housed with their own tenancies, often in hard-to-let flats. Some centres felt that this mixture was of positive benefit: people who were housed could serve as an example and pass on information to those who were not.

In practice, centre staff had to prioritise particular groups, and opinion was also mixed among users as to whose needs should be catered for. For example, people sleeping out often felt that those housed were in far less need: 'these places should be for people who are really homeless.' People who were housed often felt worse off than they were before, in every sense, and that day centres should therefore continue to meet their needs. Some people argued that because they had not encountered many women or black people using single homeless institutions, there was no need to provide services for them.

People's expectations of or usage of centres were influenced by their housing situation. Describing sleeping out: *'you're dying for the place to open so that you can have a shower, clean gear to wear and something to eat, so that you can then prepare psychologically for the rest of the day'*. Someone housed describing isolation: *'this place is my second home. I'd be lost without it, staring at the same four walls'*.

The Central London Outreach Team report found that nearly 20% of their street contacts were housed but continued to identify with the street culture because they were financially poorer, and because they felt lonely or misplaced where they were living. At least 66% of their sample used day centres, which were very much part of the culture.[7] The transition from street homelessness to being housed was experienced by centre staff and users as a slow and difficult one, with many people giving up their tenancies and returning to a lifestyle that was at least familiar. *'When you're homeless, people don't want to know you and they still don't want to know you when you move in next door'*.

On the whole, centre staff saw people who were housed as being at risk of homelessness through poverty, boredom and isolation, and some stressed the importance of their preventative role, if only in helping people to get by materially. Some, like the Deptford Centre, specifically tried not to 'value judge' or impose time limits on how long people needed to use their services. Many staff referred to the length of time that could be involved before some users even approached them about housing.

Sometimes the media and the rest of the voluntary sector compounded the problems of housed people using centres. Minshull Street Day Centre 'spent two months mopping up', after the Christmas bonanza of treats for the homeless had provided a more attractive alternative to tenants otherwise facing the prospect of a cold, lonely or hungry holiday. Many people gave up their tenancies, and, on the most basic level, people were sick for sometime because of the sudden influx of rich food.

Centre staff felt that funders failed to recognise the problems involved in the housing and resettlement process, and also set unrealistic targets in the face of a widespread dearth of good quality, affordable accommodation with appropriate community support and adequate benefits and income levels. Centres could not simply process people into housing and expect them to cope, in the face of widespread discrimination by the community.

On all levels, day centres are involved in the effects of discrimination by the community towards single homeless people. Users also discriminate against each other because single homeless people are not a body of people supporting each other in a common cause. Day centres do not constitute a network of services that share the common goal of empowering users and challenging discrimination. Competition and survival of the fittest are more in evidence than communality, reflecting the general state of the voluntary sector and society at large, after a decade that rewarded materialism at obvious cost to social justice and equality. While these values prevail and there are no strong movements to challenge them, the concept of community and community centres will remain fantasy.

CHAPTER 4
Resources to fulfil aims
Funding, staffing and buildings

The core concepts of day centres as safe havens and as communities, or bridges to community, are fraught with philosophical and everyday difficulties. They are further compromised by the political and economic marginalisation of day centre staff and users, and the fact that resources available to both are distressingly inadequate. This chapter looks at how resources impinge on aims and practice.

Day centres essentially offer a building, workers and open-ended support, ranging from the direct provision of basic services to resettlement in the community. Their minimum requirements are three-fold:

- commitment by funders to a secure base for revenue funding
- access to adequate levels of skilled and experienced people
- good standard premises with adequate facilities.

FUNDING
Monitoring/evaluation
'Collecting statistics is inimical to the heart and ethos of our work' (centre manager).

'We feel pressured to fulfil a role which is surely the responsibility of either social services or health authorities and that pressure is increasing' (centre annual report).

Monitoring and evaluation of services serve a two-fold function:

- enabling staff to review and develop services and aims, so that these are responsive to users' needs
- identifying information necessary to funders in order to lobby for more resources, so that the statutory and voluntary sectors can jointly meet gaps in provision.

Where day centres did not monitor usage, it was often because this was felt to be intrusive and counter to the safe haven/community ideal, and impractical because of high numbers of people seen. Centres that undertake monitoring and evaluation felt that funders did not have a proper appreciation of their work or of operational constraints, and also that funders only appeared interested in numbers of people seen and seen to be processed into housing, employment and so on. Their monitoring forms were often more appropriate to residential projects, and they failed to take account of process and concentrated instead on outcome.

Staff frequently referred to the length of time it could take to work with individual users to any tangible effect. Firstly, dependent on the degree of institutionalisation, as well as the accessibility and resources available to the service, it could take a long time for a user to have trust or confidence in a worker and to feel safe in asking for support. Secondly, if some users simply wanted to use a centre for a cup of tea and a shower, that was an outcome as valid for that individual as finding accommodation or employment was for another. Thirdly, centres did not have magical access to dwindling housing and community resources: finding users appropriate housing and support was a time-consuming, frustrating and lengthy business. But from the perspectives of management committees or some funders, time spent by workers outside the building could appear to be a reduction in services provided, because numbers would have to be reduced, opening hours curtailed or more staff employed.

'We discourage staff from thinking in terms of success or failure but as a process...we are building a wall in the dark' (centre manager). Projects were asked how they defined and measured success or outcome. Responses were diverse and, in some instances, contradictory. For example, a measure of success was whether a user returned and continued to use a service. It was equally a measure of success if a user appeared to take greater control of her/his life and stopped using the service, or used it less frequently. Similarly, outcome could be someone saying 'hello' for the first time, or appearing to mix more with other users. Or it could be a user taking part in a job club and going on to find work; or preventing eviction by helping with welfare rights advice, or simply serving meals while a user waited for benefits to be sorted out.

Some centres had found ways to monitor services without denying the importance of process. Provided the information required was relevant to the exercise and the reasons clearly explained to users, collecting information from or about users was not offputting or unwelcoming. Some centres collected information on the whole current user group on a regular periodic basis, which avoided day-to-day difficulties, but which provided comparable data to assist in planning, and in funding applications. Funders require, for example, information on equal opportunities, and many centres do not even monitor gender. Centres undertaking advice work need certain basic information in order to provide an effective service, such as housing history to prove a local connection, or medical history to prove vulnerability. Monitoring systems included:

- numbers and breakdown of people using different aspects of the service, for example, take-up of meals, activities or programmes, advice

- an annual users' survey to: collect information on the profile of current users, and to consult with users on where current services could be altered, extended or improved
- specific surveys undertaken to inform planned developments, such as moving to new premises, or introducing an outside service to the building
- initial interviews or form-filling with all new users
- formal mechanisms for feedback from users about programmes and activities via meetings, questionnaires, quarterly reviews and so on. This could incorporate the experiences of outside agencies involved in sessional work
- records kept of advice requested and outcome where known

Projects that collected information on a regular or systematic basis, which incorporated various aspects of services offered, were in a far better position to review and plan internal services, and to identify gaps in their own and in other agencies. Day centres are well placed to monitor trends in groups affected by homelessness, and should be in a position to lobby for other services to undertake their statutory responsibilities, or to increase their accessibility to homeless people. Rather than continue to be the dumping ground of the rest of the world, centres have a role to play in passing information to co-ordinating policy and campaigning bodies that is as important as that of the residential sector.

The impact of funding on practice

'For too long day centres have been the Cinderellas in terms of funding and recognition of the work undertaken' (centre worker).

'No money from statutory bodies other than heaven' (church centre worker).

Day centres face the problem of not having a secure base of statutory revenue funding, in order to consolidate and improve current services, and to extend them where appropriate. Residential projects can at least be funded on a per capita basis, according to a quantifiable number of bedspaces. Day centres see people on an open-ended basis, and often without what funders would recognise or define as a quantifiable outcome.

Capital costs are also a problem for building-based services. The need for a cyclical maintenance and refurbishment programme for the upkeep and improvement of buildings is acknowledged in funding of the residential sector.

If day centres have to find ways to monitor and evaluate, funders also have to be prepared to acknowledge the skills, time and complexity involved in improving the access of homeless people to the community. Repeatedly, management and staff felt tied up with the day-to-day running of the building, rather than on building up the networks necessary to refer users on to. Alternatively, centres would chase money for particular aspects of service delivery, such as housing resettlement or outreach work, and then find they had to continue raising funds for the core as well as the ever-expanding service.

It was fairly common for day centres to expand into becoming housing providers because of funding availability. Statutory funders often prioritised residential services over daytime ones, and this undermined development or upgrading plans. SASH had wanted to pursue a community resource centre model and had recruited staff on this basis, but were unable to proceed because of a funding-led decision to prioritise direct access accommodation. Minshull Street faced a similar problem just at the stage when they were moving away from the 'daytime dosshouse' style and trying to provide a more proactive service to users. Priority was given instead to developing a new service, offering residential and daytime support to particular groups of homeless people. The people involved in both centres obviously felt marginalised by their umbrella organisations, but the decisions threatening closure were both forced by funders and reflected funding priorities.

Some day centres received no statutory funding: these tended to be church concerns offering basic services. All centres were dependent, to varying degrees, on funding and donations from non-statutory sources, such as private trusts, churches and public appeals. Fundraising was an increasingly time consuming task. Those centres with paid staff engaged to do fundraising and finance work were obviously more likely to fundraise effectively. Resources attracted more resources. Funding was therefore very unevenly distributed between centres.

Those outside London felt and were largely excluded from central government initiatives. Within London, centres saw resources being concentrated on the central areas, where there is historically a high public and media homelessness profile. The London Connection in central London (referred to by a funder as the 'department store' of day centres) had to sustain an annual revenue budget of £1 million. The Southend Centre for the Homeless, at the time of fieldwork, was operating on a staff group of three workers, a broken typewriter and annual local statutory funding of £31,000.

Those projects which could generate a high profile could find, as one worker put it, that they were *'lurching from one financial and management crisis to another and creating a dinosaur which sheds one tail only to replace it with another.'*

Funders also imposed limits on the nature and function of work undertaken. Users and workers were unable, for example, to campaign or lobby under a centre's aegis because this is often identified by funders as a political activity. Centres that had identified the need to develop - for example - by providing a separate service for young people, found plans frustrated by funders who did not recognise this as a priority need.

There were instances where projects had their funding cut or threatened because funders prioritised particular groups of homeless people or had narrow definitions of who is affected by homelessness. Projects catering for less visibly homeless people were less likely to attract funds than those seeing a high proportion of people sleeping out or using hostels.

Statutory funding, where it existed, was often split between different government bodies, or between different departments of the same local authority. Centres might have to fulfil different criteria for social services and housing funding. Posts funded differently within the same organisation could lead to competing interests, in fulfilling, for example, the different expectations of the youth service and those of the Department of Environment.

There was no logic or coherent plan in the way funders viewed day centre services and allocated money. The Fanon Project received no health authority funding, although users described it as having played a preventative role in hospital re-admission; but it did receive housing and Home Office funding. Non-residential services did not fit in easily as anyone's responsibility. Where centres could provide no information about who they were seeing and what they were doing, this made it easier for funders to dismiss them.

Finally, the need to fundraise or to conform to funders' expectations were the two most commonly cited reasons for the trend from co-operative or collective styles of organisation to line management structures. Funders needed to relate to an overall boss, and imposed this as a condition of continued funding. The assumption was that collectives waste time and money and that hierarchies do not, whereas the reality was felt by collectives to be that their difficulties were more honestly exposed. Funders did not appear to assess projects impartially on the respective merits of different structures to suit aims and users' needs. Workers in collectives felt that hierarchies were imposed for someone else's aggrandisement and as a further obstacle to the empowerment of users.

STAFFING
Management structures

At the SHIL/CHAR day centre conference held in March 1991, the view was expressed that non-hierarchical organisations were better placed than hierarchies to implement user involvement or participation. Workers in collectives were honest about some of the difficulties they had experienced in this area, which included that of letting go of power. No-one claimed to be working in a structure that was open and democratic as far as users were concerned. However, workers in collectives tended to keep this as a live issue, and workers with equal input into decision-making at least felt that direct contact with users ensured representation of their views and experiences on some level. Workers had generally joined collectives because they believed in shared decision-making and saw this as intrinsic to aims to empower user groups. Collectives tended to see campaigning with users as a necessary and legitimate activity, even when they experienced similar problems as other structures in other areas of user participation.

How people felt about their work or role depended on a number of factors, such as: salary and employment conditions; physical environment; project policies, especially on violence and anti-discrimination and so on. But support, or the lack of it, emerged as a major issue. Workers satisfied with the level of support received in a line management structure tended to be working in projects that were relatively well resourced, with access to other services to refer on to, and where managers retained an element of hands-on experience and gave time to workers to talk about their work. This was the case with St. Botolph's and Brighton First Base, where the day centres were fully integrated and valued within the overall structure.

There was less job satisfaction in centres that were under-resourced, and where managers were either remote from service delivery or only involved in it because of staff shortages and to the detriment of fundraising, supervision and so on. In some cases, workers were excluded from management committee meetings or felt (like users) that it was a waste of time attending.

Day centres are no different from other voluntary sector organisations in being managed overall by a group of individuals who offer their services free or as part of their paid employment. The functioning of committees in practice depends on the goodwill, skills and time available to a small core of individuals. Workers and managers often felt that committees could not support or direct their work adequately for these reasons. It was generally felt that committees should represent people from a wide variety of backgrounds and skills, but day centres had more than the usual problems in recruiting members because they are widely viewed as non-priority services.

There was common concern about user representation at management committee level, and some projects recognised that language and structures would have to change in order to improve their general accessibility: *'We are worried that centre users tend to feel overawed by what is a predominantly professional, middle class management group, and find it difficult to participate in many discussions, especially the rather arcane ones which develop over funding.'*[1] Some projects at least passed minutes of user/staff meetings to committees to pass information upwards. Others were planning to develop users' committees, or to involve users in steering groups for any planned developments.

Paid staff and conditions of service

How we want to be treated	Not treated
use our name	harassed
with respect	rubbished
as an equal	interrupted
appreciated	blamed
valued	pressured
with patience	dismissed
as a human being	threatened
with thought	shouted down
with consideration	abusively
with fairness	ignorantly

This list, the outcome of a workers' training course, was displayed on one office wall. Workers were not saying anything very different from their users.

There were wide variations between centres on staffing levels, salaries and employment conditions. But on the whole, staffing levels were regarded as inadequate to the range of tasks and skills increasingly involved. Use of volunteers and outside services could release some worker time. But repeatedly staff, including some managers, felt preoccupied with 'the everyday mundane details' of supervising the building and running basic services, rather than in pursuing an enabling or empowering role that meant taking a more outward looking approach. For example, the effective giving of advice requires an extensive and regularly updated information bank, with time available to workers to check out (with users) agencies referred to. If centres want to improve their accessibility to a wider range of homeless people, they have to be able to provide advice and information and improve their links with potential referral sources.

Interviews with workers, and some managers, were subject to delay, interruption and a sense of urgent pressure. In the course of a fairly typical interview with a worker, he had to lock the office door and unplug the phone to create some space. Within ten minutes, guilt and anxiety got the better of him and we were back to constant interruptions from users: wanting a chat, asking him to do washing or for the toilet key or pool cues, borrowing money for a job interview and so on. Other workers also interrupted because there was no other space to let off steam or ask for advice. In another centre, as opening time approached and the queues and banging on the door built up, the atmosphere changed as workers and volunteers visibly steeled themselves for the next few hours of impossible chaos.

'Workers start out with good intentions, but they soon get pissed off' (centre user). *'Projects like this function on the goodwill of workers'* (centre worker). Users and staff were often frustrated because they did not have quality time to spend together. Where users felt satisfied with the individual attention received from staff, this was often at the expense of workers in terms of rapid burn-out and disillusionment. Users at times expressed concern on behalf of individual workers, who worked long hours under stressful conditions, with very little incentive apart from the basic satisfaction of keeping the place open. Many paid staff felt deskilled, devalued and frustrated. Apart from all the difficulties discussed under safe haven and community, there were often major problems in conditions of employment.

Day centres did not usually have access to relief or peripatetic staff for periods of holiday, sick leave, meetings or training. Individual staff members could face the choice of going in to work sick or closing the centre: similarly with taking annual leave, holding or attending meetings, improving links with other services and so on. As a result of increased numbers and levels of violence, centres that used volunteers generally felt that it was unsafe and unfair that they should take on the same level of responsibility as paid staff. It was usually considered necessary for paid staff to be available throughout opening hours. New Street had panic buttons installed throughout the building and five members of staff on floor duty at all times. This level exceeded the total staff groups of many centres.

Centres had to make difficult choices about their opening hours, and there was inevitable staff guilt about any reduction to these, with corresponding complaints from users who had nowhere else to go. There was, however, increasing recognition of the need for meetings to plan services, exchange information, undertake training and so on. Workers also needed time to follow up advice and referrals. One centre closed for one day a week for meetings and training, follow-up work, and tidying up of the building. Users could still call to pick up post or for individual appointments, and generally accepted the need for closure because they could see results that benefited them. The same centre had a complaints box for users, and a regular newsletter linking users' and staff meetings, to ensure some dialogue.

Burn-out and sick leave were frequent phenomena and an equally serious problem for workers and managers. Users often commented on the quick turnover of staff. Traditionally, day centres have lacked a career structure, or opportunities for transferable and specialist skills and training. Training was often a luxury for workers. Training courses on offer were considered to be more appropriate to residential projects: for example, residents' and not users' rights. Very few projects could afford the services of outside consultants. Workers were concerned that they were giving inaccurate or outdated advice, or could be damaging people with inappropriate or insensitive responses: *'I could be making problems worse and I have no way of knowing it.' 'I just have to hope I'm saying the right thing and that it will get the right response.'*

Workers were frequently employed without written contracts of employment or on time-limited contracts, which deprived them of employment rights. Salaries and status were perceived as low in comparison with the greater opportunities available in the voluntary residential and statutory sectors. Many centres did not have written policies with guidelines for implementation and could not offer staff and users the basic protection of health and safety or equal opportunities policies.

The recruitment of staff

Professional staff groups were often dominated by young workers because of high staff turn-over and general conditions of employment. This had implications for relating to older users, as well as for consistency in sharing skills and experience. Some centres compensated for age imbalance by recruiting older volunteers.

The multi-faceted nature of the work calls for a variety of skills and backgrounds. All too frequently, people with skills and experience in one area were required to take on other roles without the necessary training. The skills involved in organising practical activities, such as photography, are substantially different from those of advice work. People recruited to run pottery workshops might find themselves responsible for implementing user participation or increasing accessibility to particular groups of people. Even in centres where posts were specialist, job descriptions were still extremely wide. A typical job description included: advice, administration, cleaning, first aid, support and resettlement, campaigning and development, and counselling in a number of areas.

The recruitment policies and composition of staff groups had a direct effect on who used services and who felt supported by services. Users often experienced workers as middle class people, and related better to staff with an appreciation of the demoralising effects of unemployment or poverty and other stigmatic labels. Centres with a mixed staff group and clear anti-discriminatory policies were safer places for more people (staff and users) than those without either or both.

Use of volunteers

Day centres had very different policies and attitudes towards volunteers. Some simply could not function without them. This was especially true for services operating a totally open access policy to large numbers of people over extended opening hours. Some centres stated that volunteers had an important role to play and that involving people from the community was one way of increasing public awareness. In some instances, it was felt that diversity of user groups called for an equal diversity in volunteer groups.

Some projects were opposed to the use of volunteers as a matter of principle or expediency: *'Volunteers over my dead body. Not until we can offer the proper levels of support and training.'* The two other main arguments were that: volunteers should not be used to replace paid staff and let funders off the hook; or that experience had been that well-intentioned middle class people were attracted to helping the poor and needy and their attitudes clashed with the prevailing ideology of the staff group.

Volunteers interviewed were as varied as any other group in day centres. Some wanted to be left alone to get on with specific tasks and to have minimal involvement in decision-making. Others very clearly were unsupported, had little idea of what was expected of them, and wanted to be consulted more by staff and committees. There was a pattern in some centres of volunteers going on to become paid staff, either through competing in open recruitment or - more commomly - as an automatic process. Those interviewed experienced the change as difficult in some way: *'When I was a volunteer, I could be nice to people. Now I spend most of my time saying no.'*

There was increasing recognition that volunteers needed support, training and status within the organisation. Most centres could not offer these to desirable standards, but some were taking steps towards these. Examples included:

- the production of volunteer handbooks
- written policies on recruitment, induction and support
- the delegation of volunteer co-ordination to specific paid posts.

Acton Homeless Concern organised social events and relaxation sessions for volunteers.

Although 'befriending', listening to people and interaction with users outside the centre were all considered appropriate roles for volunteers, no day centre had adopted formal mechanisms for support in the community, such as the practice of 'buddying' by HIV/AIDS services.

Some projects positively encouraged users to become volunteers, usually in the running of basic services. Some required users to have a time break before taking on a new role; others saw volunteering as a way for users to raise self-esteem or increase skills. Projects were as divided on this issue as they were on the concept and practice of volunteers in general.

Outside services

There was a similar debate on the use of outside services, which also depended on the nature of those services. Some projects resisted on-site medical surgeries as contributing towards a self-contained ghetto. Others saw such provision as a practical response to people who would not otherwise have access to mainstream services and as a way of bridging the gap between centre and community: *'the provision of on-site services is the first step to empowerment'* (centre manager).

External sessional workers varied in their responses to working in day centres according to a number of factors. Emmanuel House encouraged links with a wide range of outside services. Workers engaged in sessional work inside the building were invited to attend staff meetings, and this helped to create a sense of common purpose. In other instances, sessional workers were unsupported, intimidated or positively obstructed in their work. A nurse contrasted the experience of working in a small scale community centre with that of working in a large missionary centre. In the latter, she was not allowed to display health education materials and her presence was not widely advertised by staff. Her colleague, a community psychiatric nurse, had been told 'we want none of your Freudian ideas in here.' Some external services abandoned their work because take-up was low, largely because users were not informed properly that their services were on offer.

Centres frequently reported difficulties in attracting the interest of external agencies and this was attributed in large part to cutbacks in the statutory sector. This was a particular problem for centres that had developed without statutory input in planning, current statutory involvement on management committees, or current statutory funding.

THE BUILDING

'Its purpose is to serve needs and not to dominate.' *'Think about the building - would you go into a cold dusty church hall and queue to talk with someone about a problem?'*

'This is space more suitable for the dead than for the living.'

'Feel free to criticise..I never thought I could work in a place like this.'

These comments were all from workers. Given that day centres are largely building-based services, or have traditionally been so, it is somewhat critical that so many workers and users were unhappy with their physical surroundings. The physical environment is the most immediate message given to people about their status. The ambience and morale in centres often directly reflected the standards or image of the building. As one user said: *'It's nice to be somewhere glamorous. It makes you forget who you are.'*

Ownership

Who owned the building was often critical to how it could be used and how the centre was perceived. At the most basic level, owners could dictate opening hours. One centre outside London could only find church owned premises and had to move three times because of the high rents charged and the prohibitions imposed on usage. Informal outreach work carried out there confirmed that church centres deterred many people from entering, and made others feel like the recipients of charity.

Owners of buildings exercised varying levels of control over services, but could impinge radically on policies and practices. A centre cited instances of harassment and failure to carry out repairs because owners wanted to convert the building to more profitable use. More commonly, owners had some say in the management of the centre. A church based centre was trying to streamline services to smaller but more representative groups of local homeless people. The local vicar insisted that the project should carry on its open door to large numbers of people sleeping out. In another case, the building was owned by a church order, on the whole helpful to the project's aims. However, the centre could not distribute free condoms or display safe sex posters and information because of the church's stand against contraception and homosexuality.

Owners also put limits on how the building could be used. Where the building was used by more than one community group, it was frequently the case that homeless people were only allowed to use certain rooms or facilities. Young users of one centre were bored with sitting around, but workers could not allow them to use the well equipped games room on site. The underlying message from many landlords was that homeless people would spoil the building for the rest of the community.

Design

The most common model was the large hall, sometimes with a limited number of rooms leading off this and often underground. This had an immediately institutional feel. Large open spaces were often dominated by regulars or the most assertive groups. There was typically insufficient space to separate out functions and groups of people. People were crowded together without privacy or choice about how they wanted to occupy their time and with whom. There were usually no smoke-free areas apart from the kitchen. Facilities could not safely or comfortably accommodate the numbers seen. Workers and users often had no space to talk quietly and with any assurance of confidentiality.

Basement or crypt centres were often poorly lit and ventilated. These effects were compounded by poor state of decor, and the arrangement of furniture in ways which minimised individual choice. St. Botolph's is an example of careful and planned redesign and refurbishment, which can alleviate the effects of being underground.

Many buildings were not wheelchair accessible or adapted for other aspects of disability.

Centre workers and users in inadequate or stigmatic buildings face four choices:
- to leave the building as it is and deal with attendant problems of low morale and risks to health and safety
- to carry out, in a planned way, the adaptations and alterations needed to upgrade services; to find alternative premises
- to limit their functions and numbers and seek to provide fewer services more effectively and comfortably to fewer people.

Where buildings were less institutional, that is, in ordinary neutral housing or purpose-built premises, interviews with users confirmed the importance of homely and pleasant surroundings. This contradicts an argument commonly advanced that homeless people would not feel at home if their physical environment is what the rest of us would feel at home in. However, a larger number of rooms with different functions could result in staff anxiety around safety, theft and damage. It is worth noting in this respect that the higher the quality of the environment and the greater the extent of user involvement in the building and services, the less the need for workers to be deployed in policing or warden style work.

There was a trend towards an annual closure for basic decoration and repairs. Some centres involved users in this work.

Building based services

Day centres have been traditionally inward-looking services dominated by the buildings that house them. The consequences of this for users and staff have been far reaching. The main function of centres is to enable single homeless people to move away from them, whereas for all sorts of reasons, they all too often contain them instead. Workers often spend their time policing and engaged in tasks that are demoralising and deskilling, rather than in building with users the links and resources that would enhance their users' prospects of leading more independent and fulfilling lives. Users with time on their hands and with skills and ideas to contribute often sit around watching workers burn out. Funders perpetuate the situation by judging centres according to quantity and output rather than the quality and process. Buildings are too often substandard, with design often unable to accommodate need, and dubious attitudes from many quarters that this situation is acceptable to and for people, simply because they are homeless.

CHAPTER 5
Some ways forward
Summary and conclusions

Time for review

Nearly all day centres contacted for this report were in the process of review. In some cases, this was the outcome of planned development. More commonly, day centres were responding on a crisis and reactive basis to growing numbers and diversity of people affected by homelessness, with diminishing resources with which to respond. Workers frequently referred to day centres as the 'dumping ground' of the statutory services, and there was common concern that they were increasingly seeing people, such as young people and people with mental health problems, who should have been receiving some assistance and support as a statutory entitlement. On all levels, day centres faced the real ethical dilemma of whether to continue and expand to meet ever growing need, or whether to put limits on services and users, knowing that there would be plenty of others left with nowhere to go.

Such dilemmas are not new and there will always be others to take their place. Back in the '70s and early '80s the residential sector, spearheaded by CHAR, had to question seriously the standards of accommodation being offered and make a commitment to hearing what homeless people had been saying for years: that they did not want to be herded into substandard buildings and treated as people of negative status. Homeless people are still saying this. Change is slow and often where one group of people make a commitment to change and closure, there is another group - very often church based - ready to respond pragmatically and open another substandard service or institution. While there are people dying on the streets, the case for pragmatism is a powerful one, as the cold weather initiatives of '90-'91 showed. However, pragmatism undermines idealism and gives the government cheap and short term solutions to homelessness.

For day centres, the closure of large residential institutions has brought another set of problems in its wake, in the absence of enough replacement housing and community support. Day centres nationally worried about the gaps in direct access accommodation, and some have expanded into direct housing provision to fill this gap. The cycle goes on.

If there is a gap in direct access accommodation, this needs to be addressed as part of strategic local government planning around homelessness, rather than as the response of one individual local centre. There are alternatives for day centres to consider. One project identified a particular issue for current users waiting for housing with nowhere to live in the interim, and negotiated a small scale agreement with a housing association for a property to be used as a temporary base in these specific circumstances. This centre has no intention of branching into housing management, since this is seen as a separate role, and one which can come to dominate non-residential services.

It is of particular concern that new day centres are springing up in different parts of the country without a joint forum in which to discuss how to proceed and how to learn from the past. While this report is urging that we stand back and look at what we must collectively take responsibility for, more 'underground caverns' are opening to cater for visibly homeless groups and will doubtless soon discover that tea and soup are not enough. This process has to stop somewhere.

However difficult, decisions have to be faced for individual centres and for day centres as a whole, and it is clearly sensible that day centres do not face them alone, but in dialogue with each other as well as relevant local services. It is obvious that day centres would be in a better position to make decisions around development - the ways forward - if they knew each other's plans, difficulties and successes, so that there is some solid base from which to approach funders, complement housing services and become a properly resourced and integral part of a wider pattern of community care.

The current picture is one of confused and fragmented history and development, and rapid change. The impetus behind this report was CHAR's response to a cinderella service that was in crisis. Day centre staff have said that they simply cannot continue to absorb the wider crisis in housing and community, with their users having to put up with the consequences of overcrowded and under-resourced services. There is an urgent and long overdue need to agree and review general and individual roles, and standards of service provision. Now is a good time to begin this process, recognising that the network of small scale, user-responsive and empowering services is a long way off.

BRIEF SUMMARY AND CONCLUSIONS

The principles that should underpin day centre services are:
- respect
- information
- individuality
- participation
- choice.

Definitions and main concepts

Day centres are non-residential, frontline services, which share a broad understanding that homelessness does not end at housing. They offer themselves as safe havens and communities, with varying degrees of open access and open-ended support, to single homeless people excluded from mainstream services and facilities. They exist to improve the quality and opportunities in users' lives and aim to treat them with respect and dignity.

Both concepts and language need to be re-examined in relation to safe haven and community. The holistic approach and the open door would appear to be mutually exclusive.

History and development (chapter 1)

Summary

- Day centres have developed haphazardly, without a sense of common purpose and direction, and in the absence of support and recognition from second-tier policy, campaigning and funding bodies.

- Rooted in Christian philanthropy, which founded the soup kitchen, this field is still dominated by large traditional centres with substantial church input. However, there are now three main ideological types, each with advantages and disadvantages from users' perspectives. These are: place of acceptance (containment); place of change (individual rehabilitation); place of resource (empowerment).

- There has been an overall shift towards a more proactive approach to users, rather than the basic provision of food and daytime shelter.

- Day centres for single homeless people are few and far between, and users have very little choice between types of day centres, particularly outside London. Within London, most centres are concentrated in the central and West End areas.

Conclusions

- Day centres need a national forum and access to local co-ordinating bodies in order to exchange and obtain information, experience and training and to have input into strategic policy and funding decisions. CHAR has a role to play - for example - in developing this research and in lobbying for minimum standards in services, to protect the rights and enhance the status of day centre users and staff. There is evidence that second-tier organisations are beginning to take day centres seriously. SHIL involved CHAR, NFA, Consortium and Homeless Network in the organisation of two day centre conferences in 1991. The Nottingham Hostels Liaison Group and Homeless Network now employ peripatetic staff to provide some relief cover in day centres. The London

Boroughs Grant Unit is reviewing its funding of day centres. Such initiatives have to be built on.

- The future development of day centres must be more considered and deliberate. Each centre should understand its own history, role and aims, in the context of current day centre models and wider provision for single homeless people. Role and aims need a philosophical basis, which should be written down and made explicit to all current and new users. Services on offer and language used to describe these should reflect role and aims.

- New services should be planned and not simply responsive to public pressure to remove a visible problem. Planning must involve: research into local needs; collaboration with the statutory sector and joint commitment to providing resources; and consultation with potential users. This is particularly important in the light of community care initiatives.

- Single homeless people should have a choice of daytime services. Local and national planning must take account of the non-residential needs of homeless people, from advice through to leisure and immediate survival needs.

The safe haven (chapter 2)

Summary

- The target group of most day centres is impractically wide. They are not safe havens open to all any more than pubs are. Day centres see a small proportion of single homeless people, and, on the whole, cater in large part for traditional groups of homeless people with present or past experience of institutions associated with the single homeless treadmill.

- Day centre buildings often work directly against the concept of safety. Controlling the space and making it safer works against the concept of open access.

- The dominant culture in many centres is streetwise, which is based on survival of the fittest. The values of this culture are at odds with the values and perceived role of many workers.

- Day centre users expressed four main needs: a range of cheap or free practical facilities; opportunities to socialise; stimulating, enjoyable or useful ways to spend time; and advice and information. Users did not want to be patronised, preached at or done to by workers.

- All sorts of variables influence who feels at home in which centre; but first impressions, image, building, and culture are critical in determining access, subsequent usage and morale among users and staff.

Conclusions

- Each centre needs to decide who it can cater for, what it can offer and how it does this. For example, the Cardinal Hume Centre identified space as an immediate requirement of homeless families in local bed and breakfast accommodation. It provides a pleasant and spacious environment for sole use by this group at specific times.

- Improvement to the building must be considered before any other expansion to the service. The need for separate and confidential areas has to precede the employment of advice workers or outside services.

- Centres need to pay particular attention to the entrance area and the role of staff and users at that point, so that walking into a building is not intimidating, offputting or shameful.

- Centres have to limit numbers according to what is safe and comfortable in any particular building, and in order to provide a qualitative and individual service to people. Queuing outside buildings is often experienced as humiliating.

- Centre users and staff should know clearly from the outset what they do and can expect of each other. Conditions of centre usage, such as anti-discriminatory intentions, need to be explained, along with reasons and implications. Leaflets on services available at the centre and locally should be visibly displayed, with consideration given to translation.

Community or ghetto? (chapter 3)

Summary

- Single homeless people do not constitute a community as defined in this report. There are real dangers in treating them as such. The only communality between single homeless people is the discrimination they experience because they are single and homeless.

- The provision of basic practical services is important. However, day centre staff should, with users, establish links with outside services and community groups, so that their role is one of helping those who want to move on, rather than containing them.

- No day centres are operating with the full participation of their users, and it is unlikely that any existing day centre ever will.

- Centres commonly experience varying degrees of problems because of the enforced mixing of user groups. Where specialist services are offered for one group, another group often wants something similar.

- Most day centres are dominated by white men and a homophobic culture that discriminates on many levels.

- There is a climate of fear when it comes to challenging discrimination.

Conclusions

- Day centres should re-examine their role as community centres as critically as their role as safe haven.
- Users can participate more creatively in current services without a revolution.

- Centres need to work with outside groups and organisations for both on-site services and referrals outside the centre.
- Any new development, including the widening of accessibility and the provision of specialist services, needs the co-operation and understanding of current users and current staff, and support from management structures.
- There is a need for users to have access to services that are sensitive to aspects of culture, lifestyle and self-identity. Day centre workers need to consider every aspect of their service, from building, staffing composition and structure, to image and language used in their written material, in looking at equality of opportunity among users.
- Specialist and sensitive services should be considered in responding to the diversity of user groups. Separation of people and functions means restrictions to the generic open door service, unless centres plan to develop separate services for particular groups - such as the Fanon Project's plans for a black women's centre. Projects can consider dispersal models, rather than automatically thinking of building-based services.
- Day centre staff and their users will remain marginalised and divided unless they agree a common agenda, which is to challenge the discrimination exercised against single homeless people.

Resources: funding, staffing and buildings (chapter 4)

Summary

- Day centres frequently have patchy and inadequate information on their user groups and therefore cannot evaluate and review services or argue for appropriate resources.
- Funders have prioritised other services, such as advice networks and residential projects, over day centres and frequently judge them according to numbers and outcome. Conditions of funding have impinged on organisational structures, nature and function of service delivery, and target user groups.
- Work outside the centre can appear to management committees, and sometimes to funders, as a reduction in services given.
- Day centres are now almost entirely hierarchical structures, with workers and users having no input into formal decision-making structures. Problems that

74 Community or ghetto?

this can cause are compounded when centres are marginalised within wider umbrella organisations.
- Workers are commonly unsupported, untrained and undervalued. So are volunteers and users.
- Buildings often dictate rather than serve needs, and are commonly experienced by users and staff as substandard, depressing and institutional. Ownership, location, design and layout are all critical to who uses centres, how they feel about it, and what services can be provided.
- Where buildings were homely and pleasant, and where users felt involved and consulted by staff, there were fewer problems of violence and staff were less tied up with policing the building.

Conclusions

- There are ways in which day centres can monitor their services without these being intrusive or bureaucratic. Day centres should prioritise monitoring and evaluation as a matter of urgency.
- Day centres need long term revenue funding for core costs and capital funding for upgrading buildings.
- Funders and local authorities need to think imaginatively about how they can evaluate day centres and should consult with day centre staff and users. Evaluation by external bodies, such as funders and statutory services, must take account of process and the degree of discrimination experienced by single homeless people in the allocation of housing and community resources.
- Managers and committees should facilitate structures and mechanisms for the support, training and involvement of workers, users and volunteers. Training and policy organisations should design courses with equal priority given to non-residential services.
- New services should seek premises that are as ordinary as possible and above ground.
- All centres should make provision, preferably by annual closure, for refurbishment and structural alterations where appropriate. Users should be involved in any plans for improvements to the building.

This report has touched the surface of many issues that clearly need further exploration, such as definitions of mental health, the daytime needs of women, why single homeless people do not use day centres, and numerous others. Each day centre can undertake individual reviews based on some of the issues and questions raised in the text. The following were identified as priorities in terms of more large scale information gathering and research:
- local directories of daytime services, including day centres. The project profiles provide a format that can be adapted (see appendix 1)

- patterns of day centre usage, including use made and experience of other services
- funding of day centres and mechanisms for fundraising
- the role of local authorities in planning daytime services for single homeless people
- minimum standards and health and safety in buildings
- what daytime services are offered by residential projects and their development plans
- guidelines on policies in areas such as confidentiality and dealing with violence.

Closing thoughts

This is the scenario. You are homeless or threatened with it. You are officially single, and without the means or the savings to buy into the private rented or ownership markets. You should be able to find the advice, information and support you need to find housing within your means, which can accommodate changing needs and circumstances, in an area where you feel safe and accepted. Once housed, you should have access to ordinary statutory and local community resources, as well as to specialist services and facilities that you can relate to.

This should happen regardless of who you are and where you come from. You should be able to walk into, say, a women's centre, a local authority housing aid centre, a day centre for single homeless people, a residential project, and at least find out which service best suits your needs for different purposes and at different stages.

The reality is that single homeless people, unless they fit into narrow definitions of vulnerability and special need, have never been a priority in housing, social policy and planning. The reality is that day centres for single homeless people do not fit into or constitute a strategic pattern of services. The reality is that how you are treated depends on who you are, where you live in England and Wales, and the nature of your local day centre.

Of course, the power that could make any impact on whether people become and remain homeless does not rest with day centres. It goes without saying that governments should undertake a large scale, planned programme of public social housing and properly resourced and accessible community care. The voluntary sector should co-ordinate its services and should do so in partnership with, and not in place of, statutory services. Funders should provide long term revenue and capital funding, so that there is a choice between day centres that can respond in a meaningful way to a black lesbian or a white misogynist. People who use services should have a voice in determining the shape of those services which claim to empower them, and in those that are doing little more than 19th century missionaries and philanthropists.

After a few years away, it was shocking and distressing to re-enter the world of day centres, and to see the post-1979 effects of government policies on single homelessness. It came as a shock to meet so many people using and staffing day centres who felt powerless and who had little hope of things improving. It came as a shock that people who spoke out against injustice in the voluntary sector were accused by others of being simplistic or naive, because the name of the game has become pragmatism.

It is not enough to pretend that we are doing the best that we can in extremely miserable circumstances. That is not an indictment of day centre staff and their users. I met people among workers, users, and women managers especially, who were passionate, skilled and committed to ending social injustice. But I encountered frustration and disempowerment too many times to be able to write a bland report that trotted out 'comparative data' and dealt with people as if they do not really matter. I was in the position of being able to leave, and I did not have to deal with the endless and everyday grime of poverty and demoralisation and powerlessness.

Day centre staff and their users are locked in conflicts and misunderstandings with each other, and miss opportunities to identify the real issues and the real power bases and to do something together, however basic. This is hardly surprising when the whole of the voluntary sector is riddled with competition because one group or individual is empowered at the expense of another. Collective action, such as campaigning, or democratic structures that could empower users and workers are not very fashionable. Why are they threatening? To whom are they threatening?

When we are considering a fair deal for single homeless people, we need to exercise imagination, to walk around in someone else's shoes, and to try not to be hypocritical, pious or cowardly. Do building societies disqualify potential home buyers on the grounds of homophobic attitudes? Are workers, managers, funders and politicians any less homophobic than homeless people? When you want to go out and socialise, do you expect to be told how, when and with whom?

It is perhaps a platitude to talk about the exercise of imagination, and tolerance. But it does come down to how we treat each other and how we feel treated by each other; and it is a fact that different standards apply to people without those things that define status or normality, such as income and family. It is also a fact that being discriminated against does not make people more tolerant towards others experiencing different discrimination. We would all feel at home in the community if that were the case. But access to housing and support services should not be conditional, and should not mean that single homeless people put up with second class services and with being patronised by others who are earning their living, or salving their conscience, at the cost of homeless people.

We should have the courage to look honestly and critically at what we are doing to end homelessness, and how we are treating people in that process. In trying to write honestly about what I observed and learnt, it is my hope that people with the power to make any impact on single homelessness will understand better the nature and extent of the problems facing people in day centres; and that practitioners and users will recognise some of the inherent difficulties and be better informed to address these. It is my profound hope that future research and policy will be undertaken by people who can speak with personal understanding and with authority about how it really is: the human face of homelessness.

This report is simply a first step towards clarifying and presenting day centre services, and issues and questions that can promote debate and dialogue. What do we mean by single homeless people? What do we mean when we use terms like community and empowerment? Why don't homeless people have a say in what happens to them? Why is homelessness not seen as a political issue?

In exercising imagination, the most important question is whether you would or do use a day centre for single homeless people out of choice. If not, why not? And what are you going to do about it?

APPENDIX 1
Project profiles

- The Deptford Centre (London)
- Emmanuel House Day Centre (Nottingham)
- The Fanon Project (London)
- Minshull Street Day Centre (Manchester)
- New Horizon Youth Centre (London)
- New Street Day Centre (Bristol)
- SASH Day Centre (Swansea)
- St. Botolph's Crypt Centre (London)

The project profiles describe the eight day centres - four inside and four outside London - that were studied in depth for comparative purposes (see appendix 2). These were selected according to a number of criteria, to incorporate geographical spread, different target user groups, and different models. The choice was further influenced to some extent by the amount of written material available from and on projects. This reflected the amount of information available on user groups, policies and development plans.

The general skew was towards centres with paid staff teams and some sense of development in terms of polices and practices. There are very few day centres in this field nationally targeted towards young people, or black people, and to this extent the sample eight do not represent the wider picture. By far the majority of services would appear to be generic and open door, operating on inadequate funding levels, and often church concerns. This skew was therefore compensated for in visits to and information received from a broader base of centres invited to participate (see references).

The profiles describe the day centres when they were surveyed in August 1991. Inevitably some information may since have changed.

The Deptford Centre
Speedwell Street, London SE8 4AT

Aims and objectives

The Deptford Centre aims to be 'a multicultural resource centre for single homeless people offering a range of high quality services under one roof'. Access to housing (linked with unemployment and poverty) is central to the project's philosophy, as is the commitment to 'establish a service which challenges the traditional stigmatisation and segregation of single homeless people'.

Aims further include the centre's development, within the local and national context, of a strategic pattern of provision of services to single homeless people.

Three major objectives 'should inform all discussion on policy and practice at the centre':

- equality of access (including groups 'traditionally denied access to day centre provision')
- user control ('we should focus not only on acting on behalf of single homeless people, but also on enabling them to act to change their own situation')
- integration with the local community, in order to provide useful services, raise awareness and avoid segregation.

History and development

The proposal for a day centre emerged from discussions in the Deptford Forum on Single Homelessness in 1982, in response to the problems of homelessness in South East London. The Urban Programme funded three workers from September 1984, to develop and research the new centre, secure funding and run an interim service.

Just prior to its abolition, the Greater London Council (as part of the replacement money for the closure of a large local direct access hostel) provided the main impetus for capital grants to build London's first purpose-built day centre for single homeless people, opening in February 1988. The project has never secured sufficient revenue funding to meet original target staffing levels (eight full-time workers), and consequently has never opened five days a week.

The project faced a staffing and funding crisis earlier this year, when the London Borough of Lewisham withdrew part of its grant, and the London Boroughs Grant Unit threatened to axe its funding. The Deptford Centre won its appeal to the London Boroughs Grant Unit, but has been severely under-staffed. Funders' criteria were that the centre should be seeing up to 100 people daily, and should be focused on street homeless people.

The Deptford Centre

USERS

Target groups

Single homeless women and men. 'The definition of homeless is a broad one and covers all people lacking secure accommodation suited to their needs.' The project has always tried to target services towards 'hidden homeless' groups, especially in the local community, including women, black/ethnic minority groups, gay men and lesbians etc. To this end, services include translation and interpretation (particularly geared to the local Vietnamese community).

Current user group

Drop-in: women up to 25%. Advice service: women up to 47%. Drop-in: black/ethnic minority up to 25%. Advice service: black/ethnic minority up to 45%. At least 10% of users are lesbian/gay. A higher proportion of people under 25 use the advice service than the drop-in.

Housing situation of users

At least a third of centre users are in own tenancies. The project sees work with this group as positively preventing homelessness ('we do not value judge how long someone needs our services'). The centre increasingly sees people with experience of the traditional homelessness circuit, but has always tried to be accessible to groups otherwise not catered for.

Number of daily attenders

Up to 40 people use the drop-in. 1990-1991 monitoring figures for the advice service show that 94 cases were effectively completed and closed, i.e. rehoused.

User participation

Users' meetings. Users' right of representation at management level via sub-committees. Users encouraged to welcome new callers to the centre and to take responsibility for the building. Users encouraged to support each other outside the centre.

SERVICES

Opening hours

12-4pm, Mon. 10.15am-2.15pm, Tues, Thurs. The advice service runs concurrently with the drop-in. Other sessions, and individual appointments, occur outside

The Deptford Centre

normal opening hours. When staffing levels improve, the centre will extend opening hours.

Introduction to centre
Agency and self referral. A reception worker welcomes all new users, who fill in an anonymous monitoring form. Services offered are explained, along with the centre's Charter of Use, which sets out the rights as well as the responsibilities of users. Range of publicity material (some translated) available.

Facilities
Cafeteria: lunch with vegetarian option and different cultural menus (low charge). Kitchen for self-catering. Left luggage storage. Showers. Laundry. The building is purpose designed and has disabled access throughout, including lift, ramp to front door, disabled toilets and showers, and car parking facilities. The building is furnished and maintained to a high standard. There are plenty of no smoking areas and display materials.

Recreation
TV. Garden. Aikido. Range of exercise equipment. Arts and crafts (geared toward home management). Library.

Level of support
External services include: LEAP (Linked Employment and Accommodation Project) sessions, to be taken over by centre; community nurse; health authority mental health team; local drugs counselling group (tranx support); health authority drugs homeless team; local women's centre.

Housing advice/resettlement
A high priority for staff, and includes advice to local statutory and voluntary agencies. Advocacy is an integral role. The project plans to develop outreach and resettlement services and to build up access to a range of housing options. Every effort is made to keep users informed of their housing applications when they are not drop-in users.

POLICIES AND STRUCTURE

Rules and banning
The Charter of Use outlines users' rights and the following responsibilities: to respect other people's rights to use the centre; to use the centre in a non-violent

The Deptford Centre

way; to behave in a way that does not discriminate against any individual or group who uses the centre; not to act in an intimidating manner. This includes not bringing alcohol or drugs into the building. No children or animals.

Equal opportunities
Written equal opportunities policy. Staff recruited for specific skills and to represent different groups.

Confidentiality
Written policy. The right to confidentiality and privacy is guaranteed by the Charter of Use.

Health and safety
Written policy, and detailed policy on violence.

Management structure and funding
Voluntary sector; management committee with representatives from local groups and other agencies. The staffing and funding crises prompted the management committee to change the structure from collective to hierarchy, with a co-ordinator.

The project has prioritised advice, development, resettlement and employment functions. Other agencies are actively encouraged to use the building and to provide accessible services. Volunteers are not used.

Statutory funding: London Borough Grants Unit (housing); London Borough of Lewisham (social services).

Other information
From its inception, the Deptford Centre has been the subject of some controversy (and criticism) because it consciously does not fulfil the expectations of a typical day centre. The recent funding crisis demonstrated the stereotypical view of day centres, as processing large numbers of white homeless men.

Another aspect of this image problem has been the view expressed to me, by a number of professionals in the field, that the environment (Habitat furnishings etc.) is 'far too nice' for homeless people.

Emmanuel House Day Centre
53/61 Goosegate, Nottingham NG1 1FE

Aims and objectives
Emmanuel House aims to provide, above all, a social function, and to create/facilitate a 'supportive community'. In keeping with founding ideals, it is specifically non-directive and non-therapeutic: 'a place where people can rest, eat, make friends and socialise, as well as receive acceptance, support and advice.'

Although staff and external services are available to give advice and information, 'we attempt to meet people where they are, not to change them. For all of us, it is the communities to which we belong which give us our identity and sense of our value and self worth, not the provision of facilities or the giving of advice... Emmanuel House exists to give comfort, support and value to anyone who has been unable to find, or has lost, a satisfying place in the wider community.'

History and development
Emmanuel House was founded in 1976 by a 'charismatic' Catholic priest of the Augustinian Order, run by volunteers mainly from the Catholic community and provided a daytime complement to the night shelter and Salvation Army hostel. It was widely known as 'the bean factory', in reference to the standard bill of fare.

The current director, appointed three years ago, was the first woman and lay person in this post. Other major developments include: the establishment and expansion of a salaried support worker team; changes in user group, to include a more diverse range of people (especially younger men and women); networking and liaison with a wide variety of external services and bodies (including funders).

Future developments include: the opening of a separate youth centre, following a feasibility study undertaken in April 1991; dependent on funding, the opening of an evening 8-10pm club for older people in their own tenancies; the development of equal opportunities.

USERS

Target groups
'All men and women, particularly the homeless, lonely, unemployed and rootless people.' Age 16+. Increasingly services have been targeted towards particular groups/needs (women, young people, mental health etc.)

Current user group
15% women (especially in younger age group). 3% black. Significant proportion Irish/Scottish. Sexuality is not monitored. C.40% estimated to have a drink or drug problem; similar estimates for people with a mental health difficulty. A high

Emmanuel House Day Centre

proportion of younger users (under 25) are ex-local authority care and have offended.

Housing situation of users
c.15% in own tenancies. A high proportion in hostel accommodation.

Number of daily attenders
c.200. A survey in Feb. 1990 showed that the door opened 605 times in one day (once a minute in busy periods). Upwards trend in numbers.

User participation
Monthly users' meetings, chaired by staff who consult users during the preceding week for agenda items. Minutes are displayed on the centre notice-board and in the newsletter. Monthly newsletter with contributions by users. Elected user representative attends part of the monthly staff meeting. Users run the clothing store and are involved in cleaning up, laundry, food preparation and displaying job vacancies on notice-board etc. Public speaking with the director.

Users have to be away from the centre for six months before they can be considered as a volunteer or staff applicant. There are plans to incorporate user representation on the steering group of the youth centre and on the equal opportunities working party.

SERVICES

Opening hours
365 days a year from 9am-10pm. Closed Wed. pm for staff meetings. Fixed annual closure for decoration, staff holidays.

Introduction to centre
No formal referral systems - open door policy. Mainly word of mouth. Emmanuel House has a high profile in the city, as the area's major daytime resource for single homeless people. Workers police the door and will check breath for alcohol.

Facilities
Snack bar from 10am including hot lunch, tea and coffee (low charge/ voucher system). Showers. Clothing store. Storage space. Disabled access to ground floor only and one disabled toilet. The building is an old department store with the main

Emmanuel House Day Centre

eating/social area in large room on ground floor. Office space, games room, quiet room, library and clothing store on first floor. Display materials. Smoking allowed in all communal areas.

Recreation

Games room, including pool and table tennis; library; quiet room. TV pm only. Art and crafts classes. Music. Football team. Trips, parties and celebration of annual events throughout the year. Users' birthdays are acknowledged.

Level of support

Much staff and volunteer time is spent in the logistics of running basic services, policing the building and door. External services include: weekly GP clinic; walk-in service by community nurses; advice sessions and follow-up work by mental health team (Nottingham Hostels Liaison Group); welfare rights surgery (local advice centre); life skills (numeracy and literacy); health authority AIDS and drugs worker. No formal counselling.

Housing advice/resettlement

Basic assistance on accommodation is given by staff. More detailed assessment and follow-up undertaken largely through the Nottingham Hostels Liaison Group, who have a newly established resettlement team of peripatetic workers. Emmanuel House staff (including managers) do resettlement and support work mainly in their own personal time.

POLICIES AND STRUCTURE

Rules and banning

No-one under influence of alcohol or drugs (a large sign on the outside of the building reinforces this). Respect others, do not use bad language. Food, money or clothing will not be given away. Users not allowed in kitchen without staff permission. TV not normally switched on before 1pm. Users not allowed to use phone to make or receive personal calls.

In an incident of fighting, both parties will normally be expelled. Users cannot leave personal possessions in office. 'Anyone flagrantly abusing the above rules or causing damage to people or property in the centre will be barred.' Reinstatement after ban by interview with director and/or staff.

Emmanuel House Day Centre

Equal opportunities

Emmanuel House is working towards developing an equal opportunities policy and working party. As an environment to work in, the centre was described to me as 'sexist and abusive'. It is not safe for staff or users to come out as lesbian, gay or bisexual. It is also acknowledged to be an intimidating environment for black and Asian people.

Confidentiality

No current written policy. Staff do not keep records. There is little space available for privacy: most of the smaller rooms double up in functions.

Health and safety

No current written policy - a priority for management. Violence has been a major issue for staff, which may have been somewhat ameliorated by the recent opening of a 'wet' day centre for people with alcohol problems.

Management structure and funding

Voluntary project. Building owned by Augustinian Order who are represented on the council of management (meets quarterly, with representatives from local statutory and voluntary projects and churches). Monthly sub-committee for personnel matters. The council of management has been actively involved in service and staffing reviews. No worker or user representation on council of management, although there is volunteer representation.

Hierarchy with director and assistant director. Staffing: five support workers; one part-time cook; one part-time administrative assistant. Some sessional workers. Volunteer group of 150 drawn from churches, university etc. Volunteers work in shifts of two hours from 10am-10pm.

Other information

The centre is chronically under-resourced in staffing terms, despite the effective networking with other agencies; and has been frustrated in attempts to attract statutory funding (especially from central government initiatives) just to improve staffing levels.

The high turnover of support staff (who often start in the centre as volunteers) is partly the result of quick de-skilling because, inevitably, workers' roles are mainly experienced as policing and saying no. Violence and abuse have been major problems.

The Fanon Project
Brixton Circle Projects
33 Effra Road, Brixton, London SW2 1BZ

Aims and objectives
The Fanon Project is philosophically rooted in the theories advanced by Franz Fanon, who clearly linked the labelling and treatment of black mental health problems to wider economic, political and social deprivation caused by Western racism. Homelessness and inequitable access to housing are part of this process.

The project's philosophy 'is based on providing services of alternative therapy to assist in the reduction of alienation, isolation and condemnation of users. The Fanon creates an environment which is stress-free, safe and secure for users to visit on a daily basis rather than wandering the streets and not receiving the proper help and support they require. The project enables the users to maintain independent living in order that they may cope with the community as it exists.'

The centre encourages self-help and the development of appropriate networks. It strives to provide a non-medical alternative to mainstream services, thereby empowering people by giving them a choice.

History and development
The Fanon Project is part of Brixton Circle Projects, which otherwise comprises a six-bed special needs housing scheme for black women who are homeless or inadequately housed. It was founded in 1984, after the Scarman Report highlighted the incidence and prevalence of black people 'wandering the streets of Brixton in need of housing and other services'. Local research supported this.

The Fanon Project replaced Brixton Circle Projects' Evening Club, which had been a drop-in service geared towards homeless/inadequately housed white men. Brixton Circle Projects is proceeding with a 21-bed residential project for black people with a mental health difficulty, and a separate day centre for black women.

USERS
Target groups
Black (Caribbean) people who have been labelled with a mental health problem. 18-60s.

Current user group
10% women. 30% referred by probation service. Sexuality is not monitored. The culture is predominantly male heterosexual. Very small proportion of Caribbean Asian users.

The Fanon Project

Housing situation of users
C.25% homeless or inadequately housed. C.75% in own tenancies (often through Fanon Project). Most users would prefer to be street homeless, in squats, or staying with friends, than use hostels, bed and breakfast etc, which are experienced as 'institutionally racist'.

Number of daily attenders
40-50. Two to four new referrals weekly. Over 300 people on referral register. Upwards trend in referrals, although upper limit for people in building is 50.

User participation
Fortnightly centre meetings with staff present. User representation on management committee (implemented). User representation at part of staff meeting. Review of groups to incorporate user feedback for planning of future sessions. User self-help encouraged (e.g. welcoming new callers to centre; visiting each other outside the centre; defusing potentially violent or tense situations in the centre).

SERVICES

Opening hours
11am-4pm, Mon, Wed, Thurs, Fri. All parts of service open during these hours. Provides 'a loosely structured programme of activities'.

Introduction to centre
Self and agency referrals (probation, social services, hospitals, GPs etc.) A worker interviews individuals referred, to explain services offered, and to assess needs and how to meet these. No reception area: intercom system.

Facilities
Caribbean lunch (low charge); tea/coffee. Shower and laundry. Library. Building is a five floor terraced house, with no disabled access or facilities. Different activities take place in separate rooms, which is problematic for disabled access, but gives the project a less institutional feel than the standard large hall of many centres. Some offices are no smoking areas. Display information/posters.

Recreation
Table tennis; snooker; TV and video; quiet reading room; darts; music room. When available, external tutors offer sessions in art, photography, sports etc. Outings subject to funding. Gardening.

The Fanon Project

Level of support
Project offers individual counselling and short-term groups such as relaxation. Works with outside agencies and family members where appropriate. Advocacy seen as important role. Liaises and encourages around education and employment.

No direct provision of primary health care: 'by maintaining the social welfare of a human being, we believe we are preventing a lot of problems.' Lambeth Social Services black occupational therapist visits weekly.

Housing advice/resettlement
Fanon Project workers use the housing manager separately employed by Brixton Circle Projects as a resource. Some housing association nominations. Resettlement largely undertaken by social services occupational therapist. Users are encouraged to visit each other in hospital, at home etc.

POLICIES AND STRUCTURE

Rules and banning
No alcohol/illegal substances on premises. No violence to each other, to staff, to the building. No medication to be given on the premises. No children. Have only banned two people in two years. Will offer contact, on request, to people banned, who may be offered an appointment but cannot use the centre's facilities.

Equal opportunities
Equal Opportunities Statement of Intent. Staff team mixed in terms of gender and mainly black. The centre is acknowledged to be inaccessible to most women, and to out lesbians, gay men and bisexuals. The Fanon Project is pursuing a Lambeth council backed proposal to establish a day centre, exclusively for black women with mental health problems.

Confidentiality
No written policy but workers adhere to recognised guidelines. Office space will be made available for private interviews/counselling.

Health and safety
Written policy, including HIV and AIDS. Written policies on management of violence. Upper limit of 50 in building.

The Fanon Project

Management structure and funding

Voluntary project/hierarchy with a management committee.

Staffing: Four full-time project workers (preferably with social work, nursing or mental health backgrounds/qualifications); one full-time cook; one part-time cleaner. Project currently working on recruitment, induction and support programme for volunteers.

Statutory funding from: London Borough Grants Unit; London Borough of Lambeth; Home Office.

Other information

Workers describe this as the only day centre of its kind in the country. The day centre workers are currently paid substantially less than the housing management posts in the project.

Minshull Street Day Centre
Greater Manchester Probation Service - Homeless Offenders Unit
12 Minshull Street, Piccadilly, Manchester M1 3DR.

Aims and objectives
Minshull Street Day Centre retains the four original aims with which it was founded in 1975:
- 'to provide physical comfort and shelter
- to act as an advice and referral point for a variety of problems
- to encourage the making of relationships between users, staff and volunteers in a friendly and informal atmosphere
- to offer some activities in the centre.'

As part of Greater Manchester Probation Service, the day centre is aiming to support people in the community and to reduce the likelihood of re-offending, but its overall role and user group are both wider than this. It is the only day centre in Greater Manchester that is not approved for use under Schedule 2 of the 1982 Criminal Justice Act (compulsory attendance under a court order). Publicity material states that 'we are attempting to run a range of activities to challenge and encourage self-esteem. This hopefully leads to some clients wanting to be directed to education, work and training or just the more rewarding use of their time.'

History and development
Minshull Street was established in 1975 in response to the public visibility of men living mainly in large Victorian hostels in the city centre, which operated curfews. Apart from the years when Community Programme workers were available (ended 1987), staffing levels have remained the same for many years. This, combined with changes to the probation service, prompted a review of the centre in 1987, with bids for increased staffing unsuccessfully made in the next two successive years.

The ethos and style of the centre have been found to be incompatible with organisational criteria for evaluating service delivery and measuring staffing levels. A further review was undertaken internally and completed in January 1991. This found that the centre, especially with its new emphasis on activities, was providing a useful service.

The probation service has decided to withdraw its involvement and staff from the centre as from October 1992; and is involved in the opening of a new project which will combine day centre, detoxification centre and bedspaces for a limited number of homeless people with a drink/drug problem. Other organisations are being invited to take over the building and running of the current day centre.

Minshull Street Day Centre

USERS

Target groups
'Anyone over 17 especially the single homeless and rootless.' A research survey (Jan. 1991) found that 70% of users sampled had convictions, with almost 60% having served a prison sentence. Women-only groups.

Current user group
c.10% women. 1% black. 70% of users described themselves as having problems related to depression, loneliness or both. Sexuality not monitored. The environment is acknowledged as intimidating to women, and to gay men, lesbians and bisexuals. Upwards trend in numbers of young people: in 1990 46% aged 17-35.

Housing situation of users
Above survey found 52% in own tenancies, but this is usually low standard accommodation (hard-to-lets on large estates). 40% had given up tenancies in last five years. The centre's definition of homelessness includes people in their own tenancies 'without established roots in the community.'

Number of daily attenders
c. 70

User participation
No formal mechanisms for user involvement in management or running of service. Weekly meetings were abandoned. However, staff try to consult with users over groups and activities. User volunteers run the laundry and clothing store. Users help to police the floor. Volunteers and users have campaigned against the closure of the centre as a probation resource.

SERVICES

Opening hours
9.30am-4pm Mon-Fri. 10am-2pm Sat.

Minshull Street Day Centre

Introduction to centre
Open door policy - no formal referral systems.'Most agencies in the city know of our existence.' Most newcomers hear of the centre through word of mouth. Publicity material available. (The survey found that area probation officers were often unaware of the centre's current services).

Facilities
Snacks, lunch, tea and coffee (low charge). Clothing store. Laundry facilities/iron. Shower. No disabled access or facilities. The centre is in the basement of the Homeless Offenders Unit and comprises one large hall, with kitchen, clothing store and small staff office.

Recreation
Pool tables; art/crafts; music; creative writing; games and quizzes; sports and outings; videos. Activities dependent on staff/volunteer availability and skills.

Level of support
Workers give advice in a number of areas (especially welfare rights), but refer to probation service for formal counselling and other resources such as employment training, and some housing advice. Primary health care: visits from community psychiatric nurse; chiropody; discussion groups and video workshops.

Housing advice/resettlement
Workers give advice on emergency accommodation. Resettlement is undertaken by the Homeless Offenders Unit.

POLICIES AND STRUCTURE

Rules and banning
No-one under 17. No-one obviously under the influence of drink or drugs and likely to be disruptive. No alcohol or drugs on premises. No animals. No children. No violence or abuse to staff or users. No racism or sexism. Rules displayed in centre. Breach of rules can result in bans for rest of day, week or month. Indefinite bans can only be imposed by the Homeless Offenders Unit.

Equal opportunities
Written policy of probation service. All white staff team.

Project profiles 95

Minshull Street Day Centre

Confidentiality

Written policy of probation service. Inadequate space for private interviewing. No monitoring except headcounts and take-up of activities.

Health and safety

Written policy of probation service. Written policy on violence (with training). No natural light or ventilation in the building.

Management structure and funding

Used to have separate charitable status (recently lost), although has always been under the umbrella of the probation service.

Staffing: two probation service assistants (not qualified probation officers); one part-time cook (not contracted). The liaison probation officer supervises staff. Accountability through probation hierarchy.

Two volunteers daily (pool of about 15 volunteers, formally vetted by Home Office, but without access to the training and supervision given to other probation volunteers). The centre is now a Community Service Order placement.

Totally funded by the probation service.

Other information

There are approximately nine probation day centres operating an open access policy nationally. A similar project - the Wayside Project (Northumbria Probation Service) is staffed by seven probation assistants and a team leader who is a probation officer. This project was cited as an example of good practice in the Audit Commission report on the probation service, 'Promoting Value for Money'.

New Horizon Youth Centre
1 Macklin Street London, WC2B 5NH

Aims and objectives
New Horizon is a youth centre in London's West End, offering advice, information and a drop-in and youth work programme on-site, and a detached advice service in Kings Cross. It aims 'to empower young people to take control of their environment and situation and to enable young people to develop their individuality and creativity.'

In stressing self-help and the promotion of a 'more positive image' of young homeless people, the centre deliberately avoids what staff perceive as the more institutional aspects of traditional day centre services, such as food, showers and laundry. In interviews, workers described the centre as 'a place where it is safe for users (and staff) to fail.'

History and development
New Horizon was founded in 1970 by Lord Longford, to work with people using drugs, and originated as an entirely volunteer project. It has undergone various and substantial changes to user group, styles of working, and staffing structure and composition: for example, from intense therapeutic group work to a non-interventionist and overtly political stance; from hierarchy to collective. Workers feel that a balance has now been struck between self-help and access to advice/information from staff and other services.

The staff team has expanded to include specialised advice, detached and campaign posts. New Horizon encourages other services to offer sessions in the centre, but rejected the on-site provision of primary health care as ghettoising.

The building, owned by private property speculators, is far from satisfactory in terms of health and safety, disabled access and confidential space, and the project is seeking alternative premises.

USERS
Target groups
'All young people aged 16-21.' In practice, users are or have been homeless and unemployed.

Current user group
39% women. 23% Black/Asian. 25% Irish/Scottish. Over 40% are ex-local authority care.

New Horizon Youth Centre

Housing situation of users
Over 50% street homeless/emergency hostel. Up to 19% in own tenancies. Project defines homelessness to include young people with support needs in their own tenancies.

Number of daily attenders
Average 48 as at 31.3.91. Minimum 20, up to 80. Some users may only use advice service.

User participation
This is currently under review, with the aim of improving formal mechanisms, partly in response to some users' requests for more participation. Weekly centre meetings for whoever is in the building, including youth workers. Chaired by a user, with an open agenda with items from both users and staff. Not minuted. Theoretical representation on management committee - in practice this does not happen. Involvement of users in direct action/campaigning.

SERVICES

Opening hours
10.30am-5.30pm, Mon, Tues, Thurs, Fri. 1pm-5.30pm, Wed. Activities, groups and appointments operate am. Drop-in and open advice sessions operate pm.

Introduction to centre
No formal referral system. Word of mouth and agency (especially Centrepoint). Publicity leaflet available but not widely disseminated. Worker on door. Two workers in drop-in, who try to introduce new callers to the centre.

Facilities
Tea/coffee free. Newspapers. No disabled access/facilities. Social area for drop-in upstairs room. Separate rooms for art, music, advice and staff offices. Small room for private interviews. No smoking area in advice room. Display information/posters

Recreation
'We do the things a youth club traditionally does.' The youth work programme includes: swimming; weight training; canoeing; video making and viewing; art/photography/music workshops; a magazine group; discussion groups etc. The social area has card and board games and table football.

98   Community or ghetto?

New Horizon Youth Centre

Level of support
Advice, or access to information/services on: employment; welfare rights (including legal advice); further education/training. Will obtain free birth certificates and medical cards for ID. Informal 'counselling' takes place, but workers are not trained in this area and will refer on. Some advocacy. Campaigning.

Housing advice/resettlement
One advice worker specialises in housing. The project has access to some housing association nominations, and to the Private Sector Leasing Scheme through membership of Homeless Network (homelessness co-ordinating body for central London). The numbers of young people housed have increased considerably with the latter scheme. Will house anyone using the centre, including first time callers. Resettlement work, including home visits, now undertaken.

POLICIES AND STRUCTURE

Rules and banning
No violence. No alcohol/drugs in building. No threatening, bullying or aggressive behaviour. No offensive language. No offensive clothing. No-one over 21 (ID can be requested at the door). No pets in building or chained outside. No more than one person in toilet. No graffiti. No-one who has been drinking or taking drugs. Bans can be immediate. Verbal warnings usually precede. Appeal against banning can be made in writing to the chair of the management committee. New Horizon sees a lot of young people who are banned from other youth services.

Equal opportunities
Separate groups for women, and for lesbians, gay men and bisexuals. Attendance of these group fluctuates, with numbers generally low. Written equal opportunities policy. Staff team recruited to represent mix in gender, ethnic origin and sexuality. It is felt that this has had a direct impact on a more mixed user group. Project cannot 'deal with behavioural difficulties' - overt mental health problems. Increased awareness of issues around sexuality, but user culture generally homophobic.

Confidentiality
Written policy.

Health and safety
Written policy, including HIV and AIDS. Written policy on management and prevention of violence at work. Increasing levels of violence have been reported by staff (as in other central London agencies).

Project profiles 99

New Horizon Youth Centre

Management structure and funding

Voluntary project managed by management committee that meets monthly and includes some members from opening days. The management committee recently decided to change the project structure from a collective to a hierarchy with a director's post.

Staff team currently comprises: Four youth workers; two advice workers (employment and housing); two detached workers; one campaign worker; one finance/fundraiser; one co-ordinator. Volunteers are not used as a matter of policy. New Horizon employs part-time sessional workers.

Statutory funding from London Boroughs of Camden and Westminster; Home Office; DION (Irish Government); London Boroughs Grant Unit.

Other information

New Horizon shares many of its user group with the London Connection, situated nearby and offering more traditional day centre facilities (a cafe, showers, medical room etc.) for young people aged 16-25.

There is some consultation between the two centres over opening hours, the timing of groups, banning policies etc, but the two centres have distinct styles of working and ethos. New Horizon believes that consumer choice is an important principle, and resisted being absorbed into the London Connection when this was being established as a new service.

New Street Day Centre
Bristol Cyrenians
1 New Street, St. Judes, Bristol BS2 9BX

Aims and objectives
Bristol Cyrenians is a major primary resource for single homeless people in Bristol and Avon, offering four services: a range of supportive housing projects; a day centre; an outreach team; and the recently developed resettlement service.

Within the wider organisational objective to provide a range of high quality services to homeless people, the day centre has two core aims:
- to offer basic services/amenities to meet immediate survival needs
- 'to enable and empower people (who want to) to gain and remain in permanent accommodation'. The centre endeavours to maintain a balance between these two.

The 1990 Annual Report describes New Street as 'a lively village atmosphere where homeless people can get everything from meals, haircuts and library books to specialised housing advice and activity sessions'.

History and development
Bristol Cyrenians began with a volunteer soup-run in 1969 and the opening of a shared house the following year. The old day centre was established in 1976 and was, for many years, a volunteer enterprise, providing basic services from an inadequate building. In 1984, Urban Aid funding was secured to build the first purpose-built centre for single homeless people in England and Wales.

The new centre opened in 1986 with a staff group of 25, but faced a funding crisis two years later, with the ending of the government's MSC Community Programme Scheme. It was saved by the Bishop of Bristol's appeal and went on to secure local authority funding for a permanent staff team in 1989.

Like other centres, New Street is constantly reviewing its service delivery, particularly in response to gaps in services identified. For example, staff recently decided that the centre cannot adequately cater for women and children, and is looking for ways to limit numbers, without losing completely the open door policy and ethos.

USERS
Target groups
'Single homeless people and childless couples.' The centre has services (reflected in staff specialist areas) targeted at eg: ex-offenders; people with mental health difficulties; people with alcohol/drug problems; women; young people (16-25).

New Street Day Centre

Current user group

The 1991 summer survey (sample size 92) showed the following: 22% women; 40% 16-25 year old people (10% increase on previous year); 2% Afro-Caribbean (no Asian users); 27% Irish/Scottish. 34% had a health problem; with 10% a self-defined mental health problem (a drop by 48% from the previous year); 30% with a worry about legal and illegal drug use and 30% anxious about alcohol use. Of the total user group, 34% had been in local authority care. Only 8% described themselves as 'professional'.

Housing situation of users

27% in own tenancies. 13% had slept rough the previous night. The rest in squats (4%); hostels (12%); night shelters (24%); bed and breakfast (7%); with friends (9%); travellers (3%).

Number of daily attenders

Up to 169 in am drop-in. Over 2,500 used the centre in 1990. Upwards trend in numbers attending.

User participation

An annual survey conducted in two parts: to gain information on the profile of users, to gear services appropriately; to get feedback from users on services currently provided. This information is also used to feed in to wider forums, to lobby for resources. A bi-monthly newsletter. Fortnightly users' meeting attended by staff and minuted. A users' committee was abandoned through apathy.

The increased professionalism of the service has meant that previous areas of users' responsibility (the cafe, clothing store, laundry) have been taken over by paid staff - a source of contention. Users have to be away from the centre for six months before applying to become volunteers.

SERVICES

Opening hours

Drop-in: 9.30am-1pm, Mon-Fri. Activities: 2.30-4.30pm, Mon, Tues, Wed, Fri; 9.30am-1pm, Sun. Youth project (16-30): 7.30-9.30pm, Wed. Annual closure for decoration

102 Community or ghetto?

New Street Day Centre

Introduction to centre

Mainly by word of mouth. The centre operates an open door policy in the morning, with a worker supervising the door. Afternoon sessions are structured activities/groups and have an upper limit on numbers. Publicity leaflets available. The project tries to make the entrance foyer welcoming and intends to redesign this to make it more of a reception/information point.

Facilities

Lunch, tea and coffee (low charge). Seating for up to 80 people. Individual lockable lockers and baggage space. Bath and showers with grab rails. Laundry. Clothing store (free). Condoms, sanitary towels etc. Although purpose-built, there is great difficulty getting from one side of the upper floor to the other - a problem for disabled access. Workers consider the building already too small to accommodate the increasing numbers of people seen.

Recreation

Outings, library, arts and crafts room (painting, woodwork, pottery etc). Creative writing group and newsletter. TV and video. Photography, table tennis and darts. Board games and quizzes. Bingo, sports and garden. The Youth Project 'encourages recreational activities in the community'.

Level of support

Advice sessions daily (welfare rights and housing). External services are encouraged into the centre and include: legal advice (local solicitors); community psychiatric nurse (mental health group and individual work); two nurses weekly; literacy/numeracy; needle exchange and drugs advice. The project abandoned the key worker system, but staff undertake 'one-to-one' work, which is time limited and task oriented.

Housing advice/resettlement

Access to Bristol Cyrenians residential projects, including new high-care scheme for people with mental health difficulties. Emergency housing advice through daily advice sessions. Twice weekly housing surgery for longer term work (most applications made under Part III of the 1985 Housing Act). The centre works jointly with the resettlement team on life skills training programmes and groupwork. The outreach team do initial settling-in visits, and then hand over to the resettlement team.

New Street Day Centre

POLICIES AND STRUCTURE

Rules and banning

No violence. No racist, sexist behaviour. No-one whose behaviour is likely to be disruptive through drink or drugs. No alcohol or drugs on the premises. No children. No animals (the kennels for dogs had to be discontinued because of complaints about noise). Abuse of rules normally results in a 'talking to', followed by a verbal warning. Immediate bans can be imposed for violence etc.

Equal opportunities

Written statement of intent, with working party to review as part of constant process. Staff recruited according to equal opportunities policy: sexuality recently monitored for staff applications.

Confidentiality

Staff follow recognised guidelines. Confidentiality is to the team and not individual worker. Police entry to the centre is discouraged.

Health and safety

Written policy. Five full-time staff on floor at any time. Women workers never left on own in clothing store. Panic buttons in building.

Management structure and funding

Voluntary project accountable to council of management. The staff team (21 members) is line-managed by a manager and deputy manager and comprises 10 project workers with specialist roles: three outreach workers; three sessional youth workers; four cafe workers; one maintenance worker; one part-time sessional worker. The average age of the staff team is mid-20s.

The centre has a pool of relief workers. Priority is given to staff supervision, appraisal and training but the project still suffers from staff burn-out. There are around 30 volunteers. Student placements.

SASH Day Centre
Swansea Action For the Single Homeless
21 The Strand, Swansea SA1 2AF

Aims and objectives
The day centre is part of a larger organisation (SASH) that provides accommodation for single homeless people. Its specific aims are 'to provide a range of services to homeless people and people in housing need, with an emphasis on practical support eg. food, clothing, shower and laundry facilities. Also advice, counselling, recreational facilities and life skills work, aimed at enhancing people's choices and quality of life and offering a 'ladder' of opportunities to develop personal skills necessary to maintaining an independent lifestyle.'

History & development
SASH originated in 1976 as a night shelter, in response to the public visibility of men sleeping out in Swansea. A few years later, the day centre was started as a daytime complement to the night shelter. The latter was closed in 1989 and a new 15-bed project established. This left a gap in SASH and Swansea with no direct access accommodation. The centre sees some of the people who used to use the night shelter, and who are still street homeless and 'difficult to place'. No other service is geared to this group.

The centre has expanded since it opened, to include group work, life skills and counselling. However, staffing and funding resources have been steadily eroded and the centre's future is very uncertain. Local statutory funders (Swansea City Council) have prioritised the need for direct access accommodation over daytime services. Previous plans to move premises and develop along a community/resource centre model have been shelved.

USERS

Target groups
'Primarily for single homeless people but experience shows that, amongst this broad client group, there are a multiplicity of needs.' Age 16-70. Dependent on resources available, project has tried to target specialised services as need arises (eg. women's group; mental health discussion group).

Current user group
Majority aged between 30-50. Women up to 30% (staff found that by providing a second entrance to the building, women were more encouraged to attend). Recent increase in numbers of young people seen, especially travellers. 'A high percentage have mental health problems, alcohol and drug related difficulties plus patterns of offending.' A core group of white men has been using the centre for years.

SASH Day Centre

Housing situation of users
C 25% street homeless. Small proportion in own tenancies. 'We are working with a particularly challenging client group, many of whom are isolated, lowly motivated, and have difficulties in obtaining accommodation and importantly in sustaining tenancies.'

Number of daily attenders
c.45. Up to 70 (especially in winter). Upwards trend in numbers.

User participation
'In theory, members' meeting once weekly, though it has been hard to encourage participation. They are attended by a staff member - experience shows that they do not happen otherwise.' Monitoring systems have included user feedback on services offered. Users have been involved as volunteers - in clothing store, cafeteria, running workshops. No user representation at management level anywhere in the organisation.

SERVICES

Opening hours
9am-3.45pm, Mon, Tues, Thurs, Fri. 11am-3.45pm, Wed. Access to all parts of service during opening hours. However, dwindling staff resources will reduce opening hours and services available.

Introduction to centre
'No formal referral system except for the counselling service and some of the group work programme. People hear of the centre via other local agencies both statutory and voluntary, and also largely by word of mouth.' Open door policy, but worker supervises the door. Publicity material available.

Facilities
Tea/coffee, lunch and breakfast, including vegetarian option (low charge). Clothing/laundry/shower. Portacabin building past its life span. No disabled access/facilities. Cafe/common room; kitchen and utility area; small recreational area; life skills/meeting room and TV; three toilets; one shower; three office areas, including advice room. Two separate entrances. Display information/posters. Some no smoking areas.

SASH Day Centre

Recreation
Table tennis, TV etc. Outings when possible. Used to offer varied programme of activities (recreational and educational): services now reduced to basics. Sessional workers are employed when funding available.

Level of support
Day centre used to offer structured group work programme, designed to increase self-confidence, life skills and independence. The programme was abandoned in this format, as it was found to be too structured for the user group. Staff now offer generic services, including advice and counselling. Weekly visits by health visitor.

Housing advice/resettlement
One worker specialises in housing advice, cut back to two hours daily. Appointments are kept to a minimum waiting time. Resettlement team is part of SASH overall service and operates separately from the centre. No direct access accommodation in Swansea.

POLICIES AND STRUCTURE

Rules and banning
The centre rules are displayed as a contract between users and centre. No access to people heavily under influence of alcohol or drugs. No-one under 16. No alcohol or drugs on premises. No violence. No children or animals. Respect for other people and their right to quiet enjoyment of the centre. Contravention of centre rules can result in ban - length of time dependent on circumstances surrounding decision to ban.

Equal opportunities
SASH has a written equal opportunities policy. Staff team all white women. It is not safe for staff or users to come out as gay, lesbian or bisexual. This is seen as an issue for the overall organisation, and not as particular to the day centre.

Confidentiality
No written policy. Private areas for advice and counselling.

Health and safety
SASH has written health and safety policy. Building seen by staff as 'inadequate in terms of space, design and facilities.' No restriction on numbers of users. Staff now supervise door, in response to increased incidence of drunkenness/violence.

Project profiles 107

SASH Day Centre

Management structure and funding

Voluntary project; part of wider housing organisation with director and line management structure. Team leader post for centre is now frozen. Management committee has substantial church input. Workers are excluded from management committee meetings.

Staff team reduced to: two cafeteria workers; two centre workers - each working a 32 hour week. Volunteers no longer used on grounds that: they should not replace paid members of staff; insufficient staff resources for adequate training and support.

Some statutory funding via SASH (including Urban Programme).

Other information

The centre has tended to be used as a 'dumping ground' by statutory services of 'difficult clients'. A high proportion of users have links with social services and/or probation. The centre is compromised by the inadequacy of other resources locally to refer users to, and by the nature and condition of the premises.

Whilst the rest of SASH has developed to provide better quality residential and resettlement services, the day centre has remained very much the 'Cinderella' service of the organisation.

St. Botolph's Crypt Centre
St. Botolph's Church, Aldgate, London EC1N 1AB

Aims and objectives
These are described as having three components:
- 'an individual level' - 'to provide a welcome to all our visitors; to provide a space where people feel accepted and comfortable; to create an environment which will enhance people's self-worth and self-esteem; to encourage people to think about their particular situations and to offer the opportunity and support for change to take place; to focus on people's housing needs and to offer advice and support as a means of meeting those needs.'
- 'organisational' - to develop and review services; to challenge racism and sexism; to liaise with other agencies
- 'community and national' - to participate in campaigning; to challenge stereotypes; to work with young people.

Services are split into three elements: the day centre, with a stress on individual rehabilitation and a structured programme of activities; the evening centre, with an open door policy and a stress on meeting 'the basic necessities of human survival'; and the Friday Forum, an evening run by users for social and recreational purposes.

History and development
The crypt centre started along basic soup kitchen lines in 1960; open five nights weekly and run by volunteers. The day centre opened nine years ago to offer a unique service; one that, unlike the traditional centres in the East End, was specifically not religion based, and which was alcohol and drug free. The centre also originated as an alternative to the 'tea and sympathy' approach of other centres, 'with a strong emphasis on challenging clients and facilitating change.'

Critical developments seen as : establishment of primary health care facilities; funding for a larger staff team and for tutors; establishment of 'The Lodges' (temporary supportive accommodation); funding to extend and improve the building; 1991 DoE funding to establish new Frontline Team.

USERS

Target groups
'St. Botolph's Crypt Centre aims to respond to the particular needs and problems faced by single, homeless people, or those whose needs derive from their experience of having been single and homeless.' Centre staff have liaised with other agencies to co-ordinate a network of meeting places throughout the week, targeted

St. Botolph's Crypt Centre

at women. The Frontline Advice and Resettlement Team is seeing an increasing number of women and refugee referrals in need of housing.

Current user group
15% women. 30% lesbian/gay. 5% black. Age range 17-70+. 40% ex-offenders; 50% with mental health problems; 60% with alcohol/drug problems.

Housing situation of users
c.10% in own tenancies. 90% broadly defined as homeless or inadequately housed, with c.30% street homeless.

Number of daily attenders
Day centre - up to 50. Evening centre - up to 280.

User participation
Friday Forum run by users (8-12 people) with 'informal supervision' from social work staff. 'Client helpers' - users who are 'working towards moving on from the centre' help out in the kitchen, and with administration and cleaning: encouraged to work 12 hours weekly.

Quarterly review days, with users 'working towards tailoring groups and services to their needs'. One member of the management committee is a user. Staff try to involve women in service provision. There are daily centre meetings to allocate tasks and go through activities on offer. The centre makes a point of celebrating birthdays (users and staff) as a whole community.

SERVICES

Opening hours
Day centre: 10am-4pm, Tues, Wed, Thurs. Evening centre: 6-8pm, Mon-Thurs. Friday Forum: 6-8pm. Advice and information (Frontline Team): 10am-1pm and 2-4pm, Mon-Fri.

Introduction to centre
Day centre: 'prospective users are referred from the Evening Centre and other agencies who have assessed them as having the potential to benefit from a rehabilitation programme and as being ready to change.' Initial assessment

St. Botolph's Crypt Centre

interviews of new referrals with key worker system. Evening centre has an open door policy: users are greeted at the door by staff and volunteers. Publicity material available.

Facilities
Day centre: lunch with vegetarian option (low charge), tea/coffee. Evening centre: sandwiches/tea/coffee (free). Fully equipped medical room and GP surgery. Clothing. Laundry. Disabled toilet and shower. Building extended and refurbished to accommodate increasing functions and staffing levels of project. Staff have separate office space, and there is a large room for meetings/discussion groups. The centre occupies the crypt beneath, and a new building adjacent to, St. Botolph's church and in recent years has undergone a £1 million expansion and improvement. Plans continue to improve amenities.

Recreation
Well resourced in terms of equipment and tutors, to offer a varied programme of activities including: art; photography; word processing; creative writing etc. Strong emphasis on outings, including sports. The day centre is activity based and users are positively discouraged from 'just sitting around'. Activities have a therapeutic as well as recreational intent and are aimed at enhancing the sense of community as well as self-worth.

Level of support
Day centre operates a key worker model: each user being allocated a 'social worker' for one to one work (often contract based). External services: weekly Job Club; psychologist. Evening centre: GP; HHELP team (multi- disciplinary team in East End to improve access to health care); alcohol counsellor; independent counsellor. Recently established Frontline Team offering advice and resettlement service to single people in housing need (including casual callers). Discussion groups.

Housing advice/resettlement
Department of Environment (DoE) targets for Frontline Team are set at: seeing 700 people annually to offer advice; rehousing 65 people annually. Project tries to house people according to individual need, and has some access to its 'sister' Lodge Project, which has a total of 33 bedspaces, as well as a range of other housing. Resettlement and support given high priority. The crypt is 'increasingly working with people at risk of losing their tenancies mainly due to poverty.'

Project profiles 111

St. Botolph's Crypt Centre

POLICIES AND STRUCTURE

Rules and banning

'The day centre is totally drug and alcohol free.' No animals; no children. The project's equal opportunities policy is displayed and workers actively challenge racism, sexism and homophobia.

Equal opportunities

Written equal opportunities policy displayed in centre. Staff recruited in line with equal opportunities policy, but currently all white. Aiming to become 50% gay/lesbian staff group. Separate sitting room for women, which has always been underused. Women users opposed, as stigmatising, the staff proposal to have a separate entrance to alleviate some of the problems of harassment.

Confidentiality

No written policy but regularly discussed by staff team. The social workers keep records to which users have access.

Health and safety

No written policy.

Management structure and funding

Church team separately managed but meeting regularly with centre team. Day centre team: one senior social worker; one administrator; three social workers specialising in women, mental health and alcohol (no formal social work qualifications); three project workers on 12 month contracts. Team line-managed by senior social worker. Frontline Team: one senior worker; one resettlement/alcohol worker; one resettlement/health worker; two advice workers. Placements: CQSW, Youth and Community; theology students; police cadets. Volunteer group over 100 people. Up to 10 volunteers, on a rota system, needed to run the evening centre with two social workers. Day centre staff accountable to management committee. Statutory funding: City Corporation; DoE.

Other information

Church and crypt staff work hard to generate a high profile of the centre and single homeless issues, eg. was the subject of a programme in the BBC's documentary series 'Breadline in Britain'. From a basic soup kitchen, it has evolved into a network of services, with split functions and opening hours designed to deliver a variety of services to different user groups.

APPENDIX 2
The research brief

Background

This eight month project has been an interactive process influenced by a number of factors and people. This process in itself speaks volumes about the subject matter.

CHAR, the housing campaign for single people, is a national campaign with a membership of over 750 individuals and organisations in England and Wales. It was founded in the early '70s to work with and to represent single homeless people to achieve three main objectives:

- 'to focus public attention on the housing, health and other community service needs of homeless single people
- to enforce and extend their rights to these services
- and to bring together voluntary organisations in common initiatives for change.'

The Joseph Rowntree Foundation is, in its own words, *'an independent, non-political body which funds programmes of research and innovative development in the fields of housing, social care and social policy. It supports projects of potential value to policy-makers, decision-takers and practitioners'*.

From its inception, CHAR has argued that all single people should have access to housing that is decent, safe and affordable. The last decade saw increases in the numbers and breadth of people who are homeless or threatened by it, with significant declines in public and good quality, affordable, private rented sector housing. It is no surprise, therefore, that CHAR and the voluntary sector as a whole should have focused on more housing, and more types of housing, as the main plank in campaigning, policy and research platforms. This is reflected in CHAR's change of name from the Campaign for the Homeless and Rootless to the Housing Campaign for Single People in the mid '80s.

However, CHAR's membership includes non-residential services (see objective 1 above). It was in response to the perceived crisis facing these that this project was initiated. Day centres in areas such as Bradford, Swansea and Bristol were reporting seeing dramatic increases in homeless people using their services, without appropriate levels of funding being made available to match this level of demand. Day centre staff were expressing common concern that they were not offering services relevant and accessible to women, black people, young people and people with a mental health difficulty.

CHAR recognised that *'most policy development to date has concentrated on emergency, temporary and permanent forms of accommodation or on the delivery of advice services to the permanently housed population.'* There was also acknowledgement of the enormous diversity of services in the non-residential field. CHAR therefore proposed a two year survey of daytime services for single homeless people in England and Wales. The range of services included unemployed and community centres, advice and women's centres, and potentially anywhere else where homeless people were spending their daytime hours.

The Joseph Rowntree Foundation agreed to fund a comparative case study of six centres in England and Wales. The project was still entitled 'Daytime Services For Single Homeless People' and the brief still referred to a gamut of services, using the term day centre interchangeably with these. The objectives were three-fold:

- 'to examine the different types of daytime services currently available
- to provide information on examples of good practice in the provision of services and thus to enhance the ability of day centres to alleviate and prevent homelessness
- to encourage and inform the development of new daytime services for single homeless people.'

In comparing six centres, it was proposed that the research should examine in detail all aspects of service delivery, from building and funding, to staffing and ways of working. The main vehicle for gathering this information was via discussions with staff and users of the six centres: *'we feel it is absolutely essential that the views of those who use day centres are fully incorporated into the project.'* The report was also to pay particular attention to user participation and equal opportunities. CHAR had no strategy on day centres, but intended to use the research findings to this end.

Development of the research

It is the practice of the Joseph Rowntree Foundation to appoint and chair an advisory group to oversee each of its projects. This group (see acknowledgements) largely consisted of individuals with direct experience of day centre work, with some formal research input. The group was all-white and without day centre user representation. Care was therefore taken in the course of fieldwork to address these gaps. The group advised on direction, content and dissemination of the research. In response to an initial period of consultation and interviews, the group played a major role in clarifying and developing the research brief, in order to take account of the views of people in day centres and the major issues facing them.

The report was to be focused on day centres consciously offering services in part or full to single homeless people and, in the process, work towards defining these services, as well as distinguishing different current patterns (see chapter 1). In view of its exploratory nature, and the differences between centres, the report would take a discursive approach to major issues raised and identified. It would be based on a study of eight centres in England and Wales (see appendix 1); and on interviews and literature from a much broader base to reflect the wider situation.

The fieldwork

The fieldwork took place between April and August 1991. This was a time when day centres were absorbing the impact of an economic recession, cuts to statutory services concomitant with greater responsibilities being placed on them, and a rapid succession of legislative changes and government initiatives around homelessness and care in the community. Most centres were in a process of review of some sort, in attempting to cope with the simultaneous problems of short staffing, rising numbers and the need to fundraise effectively. Some were being threatened with closure; others were springing up in various parts of the country. Given this confused picture of rapid change, the details contained, for example, in the project profiles will have changed by the time of publication. However, the report does try to highlight major common trends and constraints.

During an initial period of visits to day centres, and consultation with a range of interested individuals and organisations, a comprehensive 'questionnaire' was drawn up and piloted. This was used to gain consistent information on the eight centres that were then selected for more focused work, and formed the basis for material contained in the project profiles. Workers and managers interviewed were shown a copy of the questionnaire, and interviews were conducted around the questions and issues raised by it. It is symptomatic of the comprehensive nature of the interviews and of the pressures facing staff that collecting this information was often a lengthy process.

The amount of time I was able to spend in each of the eight centres was also dependent on timetable and budgetary constraints, as well as the circumstances and priorities of centres. For example, I was only able to visit Swansea once. In the other centres, the intention was to adapt to their style of working, according to reviews taking place, and with the aim of getting the widest possible range of perspectives. This included the views, where possible, of volunteers and outside workers such as nurses, alcohol and housing advisers, management committee members and so on.

In some centres, such as Minshull Street, I was encouraged to mix informally with users and join in whatever was going on. Others, like the Fanon Project and the Deptford Centre, arranged specific times and space for interviews with users. At St. Botolph's and New Street (Bristol), I participated in discussion groups between staff and users, which were part of the weekly programme. New Horizon invited me to take part in their staff review of user participation. Visits to Emmanuel House were arranged on days with most activity and sessional work, so that I could meet

The research brief 115

people involved in the service on a number of levels. All centres were positive about the research and very helpful in co-operating. But, because of the nature of day centres, arrangements made were generally subject to whatever else was going on and I had to be equally flexible.

Visits to other centres combined a mixture of interviews and discussions with staff and with users. Some centres were approached because they appeared to be offering unusual services, such as the women-only day at North Lambeth Day Centre. It was not appropriate to take a clipboard approach to centres and, unless there was private space for interviews or people were prepared to see me outside the centre, notes were written up as soon as possible after visits. Wherever possible, the questionnaire was used with staff in other centres to supplement the detailed information provided by the sample eight.

It would be fair to say that I largely drew on my experiences as an outreach worker and credibility as a practitioner in my approaches. By spending time in centres, often on a fairly informal basis, I was able to do a lot of observing as well as experiencing of the general atmosphere, social groupings and responses between staff and users. I was also able to approach groups on the streets or outside centres and to enlist the help and opinions of previous contacts.

These methods were supplemented by work outside centres. For example, Thames Reach Housing Association arranged a drop-in session around use of and views on day centres. This proved a useful opportunity for a range of experiences and opinions, distinguishing the different priorities of those sleeping out from those living in permanent accommodation, as well as those who never used day centres. The Central London Housing Advisory Service provided access to interviews with some women contacts living in a Salvation Army hostel.

By this variety of approaches, I was able to make contact with approximately two hundred homeless people, most of whom had or continued to use day centres.

There are very few meetings or conferences aimed at day centres although the profile of centres has been raised, at least in London, over the last year or so. Participation in the organisation and event of the second SHIL conference, and attendance at Homeless Network's day centres meetings, were further ways of hearing about some of the important issues for centres that I was not otherwise able to make contact with.

Finally, a few visits were made to other sorts of centres in order to make comparisons. For example, the Landmark in South London, which is a day centre for people with HIV/AIDS; and Hillside House, which is a daytime service for people with experience of mental health institutions wishing to return to work.

Given the dearth of secondary material in this field, the report mainly relies on source material produced by day centres. This includes annual reports, publicity material, policy documents, internal reviews and feasibility studies, job descriptions, users' surveys, and users' newsletters.

Notes

Prologue: The author, the themes, the aims

1. Adams Douglas, *The Restaurant At The End Of The Universe*, Pan, 1980, p. 158
2. Central London Outreach Team, *Sleeping Out in Central London*, GLC, 1984
3. SHIL is an all party political group, set up by the London Boroughs to bring together statutory and voluntary sector organisations involved in providing services to single homeless people in London
4. Jan Sherlock, *At Home In The Community*, Good Practice in Mental Health, 1991, p.2
5. Ibid

Introduction: Key points in understanding day centre provision

1. Philip Hope and Mik Smith, *The Feasibility Of Proposals For A Day Centre For The Young Homeless*, Housing Associations Charitable Trust, December 1985
2. Rochdale Petrus Community
3. Southend Centre for the Homeless
4. The Arlington Drop-In Centre (London Borough of Camden) was the only day centre contacted that was for single homeless people and managed and funded by a social services department. At the time of writing, this project was seeking partnership with a voluntary project in order to survive local authority cuts

Chapter 1: What is a day centre?

1. *Community Care In The Next Decade And Beyond*, HMSO, 1990
2. Cowgate Day Centre (Edinburgh Council for the Single Homeless), *Annual Report 1991*
3. Steve Phaure, *Who Really Cares? Models Of Community Care And Black Communities*, LVSC, April 1991, p.8
4. Jane Short describing the Christian Mission in the East End in 1870. Quoted in Jenty Fairbanks, *Booth's Boots*, the Campfield Press, 1983, p.3
5. Anton Wallich-Clifford, *No Fixed Abode*, Macmillan, 1974
6. Emmaus House (Acton Homeless Concern), *Annual Report*, 1990-1991
7. Society of St. Dismas, Southampton

8   The London Connection, *Annual Report 1990-1991*

9   North Lambeth Day Centre (London Borough of Lambeth)

10 Barons Court Project, *Annual Report 1989-1990*

Chapter 2: Who uses day centres and why?

1   *Week Ending*, Radio 4, October 1991

2   Southwark Day Centre, *Annual Report 1989-90, 1990-91*

3   Westside Day Centre, South Yorkshire Probation Service

4   Information supplied by the University of Surrey, 1991

5   George Orwell, *Down And Out In Paris And London*, 1933, Penguin reprint 1977

Chapter 3: The holistic approach: community or ghetto?

1   London Lighthouse was founded in 1986 by a group of people with or affected by HIV/AIDS. The centre offers residential care and daytime services

2   Stephen Anderson, The Role Of Staff At Fountain House, *The Fountain House Annual Report 1985*

3   Moran 1979, quoted in Canter et al, *The Faces Of Homelessness In London*, Department of Psychology, University of Surrey, July 1990

4   Thames Reach Housing Association, founded in 1984, provides a number of services, from street outreach work to housing for women and men sleeping out in central London

5   The Joint Forum on Mental Health and Homelessness is a co-ordinating group of voluntary, statutory and user organisations in London working in the areas of mental health and homelessness

6   The Passage, *Annual Report 1990*

7   Central London Outreach Team, op. cit.

Chapter 4: Resources to fulfil aims

1   Rochdale Petrus Community

References

Day centres visited/interviewed

(* Indicates a project profiled in appendix 1)
Arlington Drop-In Centre (social services: London Borough of Camden)
Barons Court Project (voluntary: London Borough of Hammersmith and Fulham)
The Broadway Project (MIND; London Borough of Hammersmith and Fulham)
Cardinal Hume Centre (voluntary: Westminster City Council)
Cricklewood Homeless Concern (voluntary: London Borough of Brent)
The Deptford Centre* (voluntary: London Borough of Lewisham)
Emmanuel House Day Centre* (voluntary: Nottingham)
The Fanon Project* (voluntary: London Borough of Lambeth)
First Base Day Centre (voluntary: Brighton)
Hammersmith Unemployed Workers' Centre (voluntary: London Borough of Hammersmith and Fulham)
Hillside House (voluntary: London Borough of Islington)
The Landmark (statutory/voluntary partnership: London Borough of Lambeth)
The London Connection (voluntary: Westminster City Council)
Minshull Street Day Centre* (probation: Manchester)
New Horizon Youth Centre* (voluntary: London Borough of Camden)
New Street Day Centre* (voluntary: Bristol)
North Lambeth Day Centre (voluntary: London Borough of Lambeth)
The Passage Day Centre (voluntary: Westminster City Council)
Providence Row Drop-In (voluntary: London Borough of Tower Hamlets)
SASH Day Centre* (voluntary: Swansea)
St. Paul's Crypt (voluntary: London Borough of Lewisham)
The Southend Centre for the Homeless (voluntary: Southend)
Southwark Day Centre (voluntary: London Borough of Southwark)
St. Botolph's Crypt Centre* (voluntary: London Borough of Tower Hamlets)

Written source material

(Annual reports; policy documents; publicity literature; users' surveys; internal review papers etc.)

Arlington Drop-In Centre, Barons Court Project, Bradford Day Centre (Horton Housing Association), Bridge Medical Centre (Newcastle-on-Tyne), Broadway Project, Camberwell Circle Project, Canterbury Open Christmas, Cardiff Action for Single Homeless, Cardinal Hume Centre, Cowgate Day Centre (Edinburgh Council for the Single Homeless), Cricklewood Homeless

Concern, The Deptford Centre, Emmanuel House Day Centre, Emmaus House (Acton Homeless Concern), The Fanon Project, First Base Day Centre (Brighton Housing Trust), Hammersmith Unemployed Workers' Centre, Haringey Irish Community Care Centre, Hillside House (St. Mungo Association), The Landmark, The London Connection, Minshull Street Day Centre, New Cross Circle Project, North Lambeth Day Centre, The Passage, Reading Emergency Accommodation Project, Redbridge Justice and Peace Group, Rochdale Petrus Community, SASH Day Centre, Seaview Project (Sussex), Society of St. Dismas (Southampton), Southend Centre for the Homeless, Southwark Day Centre, St. Basils Centre (Birmingham), St. Botolph's Crypt Centre, Vauxhall Action for the Homeless in the Community (Lambeth), The Wayside Project (Northumbria Probation Service), Westside Day Centre (South Yorkshire Probation Service), Whitechapel Centre (Liverpool)

Other references

David Canter et al, *The Faces Of Homelessness In London: Interim Report To The Salvation Army*, University of Surrey, 1989
David Canter et al, *Faces of Homelessness: Summary*, University of Surrey, 1991
Central London Outreach Team, *Sleeping Out In Central London*, GLC, 1984
CHAR, *The Role Of Day Centres In The Provision Of Services To Homeless Single People*, unpublished 1988
Consortium, *Provision For Single Homeless People: The Role Of Non-Residential Services*, unpublished 1984
Rose Echlin ed., *Day Care Information Pack*, Good Practices in Mental Health, 1989
Philip Hope/Mik Smith, *The Feasibility Of Proposals For A Day Centre For The Young Homeless*, report for Housing Associations Charitable Trust, 1985
Department of Health, *Community Care In The Next Decade And Beyond*, HMSO, 1990
Patrick Logan, *A Life To Be Lived: Homelessness And Pastoral Care*, UNLEASH, 1989
National Cyrenians, *Non-Residential Basic Provision*, unpublished 1982/3
Steve Phaure, *Who Really Cares? Models Of Voluntary Sector Community Care And Black Communities*, London Voluntary Service Council, 1991
Jan Sherlock, *At Home In The Community*, Good Practices in Mental Health, 1991
SHIL, *Report Of The Conference For Day Centres Held 6 March 1991*
Rick Stern et al, *From The Margins To The Mainstream: Collaboration In Planning Services With Single Homeless People*, West Lambeth Health Authority, 1989
Jo Woolf, *Contracts And Small Voluntary Groups*, London Voluntary Service Council, 1991

About CHAR

CHAR, the housing campaign for single people, represents over 750 organisations and individuals working with homeless and badly housed single people.

It campaigns locally and nationally to press government, local authorities and housing associations to meet the housing needs of all single people.

It also undertakes research into single homelessness, organises conferences and training courses, and publishes reports, guides, briefing papers and leaflets.

For further information, please contact CHAR at:

5-15 Cromer Street, London WC1H 8LS

Tel: 071 833 2071